BEETHOVEN AND ENGLAND

Portrait of Beethoven. Charcoal with chalk, 1818,
by August Karl Friedrich von Klöber

BEETHOVEN

AND ENGLAND

AN ACCOUNT OF
SOURCES IN THE BRITISH MUSEUM

by

Pamela J. Willetts

ASSISTANT KEEPER
DEPARTMENT OF MANUSCRIPTS

Published by the Trustees
of the British Museum
London 1970

SBN 7141 0464 7

Printed in Great Britain by
T. & A. Constable Ltd, Hopetoun Street
Edinburgh

CONTENTS

LIST OF ILLUSTRATIONS

PREFACE

This book has been prepared in connection with the exhibition in the King's Library of the British Museum (27 November 1970 to 28 February 1971) in celebration of the bicentenary of Beethoven's birth. Owing to considerations of space, only a selection from the Beethoven collections of the Museum could be displayed, and it was thought advisable to accompany the exhibition with a book giving a wider range of historical and bibliographical information about important material in the collections than could be included in an exhibition catalogue of more limited scope.

It is hoped that the book will be of value as a work of reference after the occasion of the bicentenary has passed. The book was largely written by Miss Pamela J. Willetts of the Department of Manuscripts, with the collaboration of Mr A. H. King of the Music Room in the Department of Printed Books, and with some assistance from Mr H. M. T. Cobbe and Mr O. W. Neighbour.

March 1970

A. H. CHAPLIN
Principal Keeper of Printed Books
T. C. SKEAT
Keeper of Manuscripts

ACKNOWLEDGEMENTS

Grateful thanks are due to Professor Joseph Kerman of the Department of Music in the University of California at Berkeley, who allowed the text accompanying the facsimile of the sketchbook, Add. MS. 29801, to be consulted before its publication: to Dr Alan Tyson for reading the book in typescript, and for making numerous suggestions: to Dr H. Ramge of the Deutsche Staatsbibliothek in Berlin, for consulting the Berlin manuscript of the Triple Concerto.

Messrs Macmillan & Co. kindly gave permission for the quotations on pp. 15, 19, 33-38, 44-47, taken from the late Emily Anderson's translation of *The Letters of Beethoven*, 1961. Grateful acknowledgement is also made to the Royal Philharmonic Society, who allowed both the quotations from its archives which are on loan to the Museum and the reproduction of one page of their manuscript full score of Beethoven's ninth symphony.

Several other illustrations are taken from sources outside the British Museum. The portrait of Sir George Smart is reproduced by courtesy of the National Portrait Gallery, and that of Sir George Thomson by courtesy of the Scottish National Portrait Gallery. The portrait of Beethoven used as the frontispiece was originally in the Musikbibliothek Peters at Leipzig, but was lost during the war. The illustration is taken, by kind permission of Atlantis Verlag, from the reproduction of the portrait in Robert Bory's *Ludwig van Beethoven. His life and work in pictures* (1960).

I

INTRODUCTION

The largest collections of Beethoven's surviving manuscripts are preserved in libraries in Berlin, Bonn, Vienna and Paris. The British Museum collections are modest in comparison, but include two notable groups of manuscripts: firstly, four autograph sketchbooks, and secondly, some interesting sources for the study of Beethoven's relations with England. The sketchbooks include a large miscellany from his Bonn period and early Vienna years and sketches for the Pastoral symphony, which have both only recently been studied in detail. The material relating to Beethoven's connections with England is comparatively unknown and throws revealing light on his negotiations with publishers and patrons. Some of the Beethoven material in the Department of Manuscripts came by gift or bequest, in particular the bequests of Miss Harriet Chichele Plowden and E. H. W. Meyerstein, but the four sketchbooks, the most important items in the collections, were all purchased.

In the Department of Printed Books the collection of editions of Beethoven's music and books about him is one of the most comprehensive in any of the world's great libraries. The catalogues of printed music contain some 4,500 entries under Beethoven's name. Among these are an almost complete collection of the continental first editions, published mainly in Vienna and Leipzig, and nearly all the important but little-known 'authentic' English editions, which are discussed in more detail on pp. 24-31.

The Department acquired several batches of early Beethoven editions in the 1930s. By far the most important of these was a group of sixty-six first and early Austrian and German editions purchased in 1936 from the duplicate stock of the Gesellschaft der Musikfreunde in Vienna. The Beethoven collection was further strengthened when the Paul Hirsch Music Library was acquired in 1946. In Hirsch's interests, Beethoven ranked second only to Mozart. He amassed well over 450 editions of his music, and of these more than half were printed in the composer's lifetime. They include many great rarities, too numerous to mention in detail. One such is an issue of the parts of the fifth symphony which Hirsch himself discovered to be earlier than any previously known. The evidence for this is in the extended pause over the tied minim in the fifth bar of the famous opening tutti of the first movement. It is the second, much more common, issue which has the pause over the fifth bar, in accordance with an early amendment by Beethoven, whereas the first issue follows the autograph exactly and has the minim pause in the fourth bar.

The Hirsch Library is also rich in Beethoven literature: it accounts for over half of the 700-odd entries in the British Museum's General Catalogue of Printed Books. Hirsch, who was a keen bibliophile besides being a practical musician, paid particular attention to books in pristine state. He owned, for instance, mint copies, in the original wrappers, of the first substantial biography of Beethoven, that by Wegeler and Ries (1838), and of the scarce Dutch translation of it (1840). Another notable book in fine state is the pamphlet on Beethoven which Wagner wrote for the centenary of 1870. Among the rarities contemporary with the composer is a copy of an anonymous pamphlet, printed at Grätz in 1811, entitled *Pastoral-Sinfonie von L. v. Beethoven*, an interesting description of the 'programme' of the work. Hirsch also collected some of the curious fugitive pieces occasioned by various Beethoven festivals and commemorations held in Germany during the nineteenth century.

In 1845, the Museum may have narrowly missed an early opportunity of acquiring Beethoven manuscripts of first importance, as is recalled by a letter preserved in the Museum from Beethoven's friend and biographer Anton Schindler to the English pianist Charles Neate. Schindler had been seeking a purchaser for the collection of Beethoven manuscripts given to him by the composer, which included the autograph score of the ninth symphony, the second Razumovsky quartet and the conversation books. Negotiations with the Prussian Royal Library in Berlin and with the Belgian Government had fallen through when, according to Schindler's account, Neate arrived unexpectedly in Aachen in June 1845, with instructions from the British Museum to examine the manuscripts. After three weeks' work Neate proposed the sum of £1,500 for the collection but had to refer to the Museum for authority. Schindler, so the story goes, was agreeable to the offer being made but Neate had to report at the beginning of August that, while no difficulties were anticipated, there would be some delay as various members of the Museum staff were on leave. The Schindler letter now in the Museum is dated 6 August 1845, and was perhaps intended to spur Neate on to further action by referring to other schemes for the future of the collection:

'A plan has been published in Cologne and Bonn to found a Beethoven Institute, that is to say a music school, in the Rhine Province, and to acquire the collection for it. . . . My wish is, and must be, to see these valuable works of art placed where they will be safely preserved for all times, . . . whether this is in the British Museum or in the Rhine Province.'

But the Prussian financier David Hansemann persuaded King Friedrich Wilhelm IV of Prussia, who had arrived in Bonn to attend the Beethoven Festival, to intervene to prevent the collection leaving the country, and the manuscripts were acquired for the Royal Library in Berlin in return for an annual pension to Schindler of 400 thaler, 200 thaler less than Schindler's previous terms which the King had declined in 1843, and less than Schindler would have received from the Museum. From Schindler's account of these transactions it seems that the negotiations on behalf of the Prussian Government were not completely straightforward and that he did not realise that he would suffer a loss by accepting the Prussian offer. It should also be mentioned that there is no account of these transactions either in the archives of the Museum or in the diary of Sir Frederic Madden, Keeper of Manuscripts at the time.

II

THE SKETCHBOOKS

The greatest treasure of the Museum's Beethoven collections is the large sketchbook (Add. MS. 29801), of which a facsimile, with commentary and transcription by Professor Joseph Kerman, is to be published in 1970 by the Museum with the Royal Musical Association. The volume is sometimes called the 'Kafka' sketchbook, after its former owner, Johann Nepomuk Kakfa of Vienna (1819-86), the composer of much light piano music, who also owned a number of other Beethoven manuscripts now in the Museum. It was purchased from Kafka in 1875: it had previously been in the possession of Artaria & Co. of Vienna, as Professor Kerman points out. Domenico Artaria very probably acquired it at the sale of Beethoven's library in November 1827. Another fifty-six leaves from the same original group as the miscellaneous London sketches are now in Berlin (Beethoven Autograph MS. 28).

Despite the implied homogeneity of its title and numbering, Add. MS. 29801 consists of two quite distinct series of sketches: the first thirty-seven leaves comprise sketches, dating from 1811, for the *Ruins of Athens*, op. 113, and *King Stephen*, op. 117; the second group (ff. 39-162) is a collection of miscellaneous leaves, preserved by chance and containing sketches, some very fragmentary, for a large number of projected works dating from the Bonn and early Vienna periods, *c.* 1786 to the end of the century, as well as autograph manuscripts of ten complete, or nearly complete, works for which it is the unique manuscript source. The *unica* include the Minuet, with sketches for the Rondo (ff. 103, 104b-5), of the wind sextet in E flat, op. 71, published in 1810, and the two surviving complete movements (ff. 119, 135-7) of the duo for viola and 'cello, WoO 32, with its teasing comment: 'Duett mit zwei obligaten Augengläsern' ('Duet with two obbligato eye-glasses'). It has been assumed that the work was composed for two short-sighted performers, and Nikolaus Zmeskall von Domanovecz, who is known to have had poor sight, has been suggested as the 'cellist. Another unique work of some interest because of its medium is the Sonatina for mandoline and keyboard, WoO 43a (ff. 73b, 87, 87b), which was written for Countess Josephine Clary, the singer and mandoline player. It was published by A. J. Hipkins in the first edition of Grove's *Dictionary of Music and Musicians*, 1880, ii, p. 205, in his article on the mandoline. An attractive work of the Bonn period, possibly the earliest work in this sketchbook, is the Romance cantabile in E minor (Hess 13) for flute, bassoon and keyboard with accompaniment for oboes and strings (ff. 74b-80b). Only the first four bars of the trio are given in the manuscript, but this section was completed by Willy Hess for his edition of the work in 1952. The Romance was probably the middle movement of a larger orchestral work which has not survived.

The overwhelming impression of this sketchbook is the immense profusion of ideas, jotted down apparently in great haste lest they be lost. Some pages are a patchwork of scraps of the most varied works. On f. 82 for instance (Plate I) notes relating to the op. 10 piano sonatas appear incongruously juxtaposed with 'God Save the King', not apparently related to Beethoven's variations on this theme, and jottings for the C minor piano concerto, op. 37, with a different Rondo from that finally used by Beethoven. Another leaf (f. 156b) has a whole maze of ideas for the D major sonata, op. 10, no. 3, including the three-note germ of the last movement scribbled at the foot of the page under the sketches for the Minuet, with the note 'Zum

Rondo'. A fair copy of the opening seven bars of the easy
G minor sonata, op. 49, no. 1, occurs at the top stave of
f. 66; it is followed, however, by a not so legible scrap of
theme from the Rondo of the Sonata pathétique, op. 13.
The second easy sonata in G published as op. 49, no. 2,
appears in far less recognisable form on f. 106, where an
earlier version of the opening of the first movement with
variant rhythm and melodic line is sketched. The verso of
the same leaf has jottings for the familiar Minuet. That
radical changes of plan were made during the course of
composition emerges from the sketch of the Rondo of the
C minor piano trio, op. 1, no. 3, marked 'Andante' (f. 139b)
as opposed to the 'Presto' of the final version, while a trio
in A flat briefly sketched on f. 59b subsequently became
the G major trio of the sonata in D, op. 10, no. 3.

Professor Kerman has drawn attention to numerous
small fragments in piano score which have not been identified as 'germs' of any known Beethoven works. He considers
these to be studies in the abstract, or notes of piano exercises
or improvisations, and not sketches for uncompleted pro-
jects. Evidence of true abandoned works does occur, as,
for example, the nearly complete rough sketch of an Adagio
in D for a piano concerto in A, dating from the late Bonn
period. This has a long note about performance (Plate II):
'In diesem adagio muss alles durchaus piano gespielt
werden nur ein einziges forte darf vorkommen. Die Klavier
Solos so kurtz und ausdrucksvoll als möglich. Das tempo
muss so langsam als möglich sein' ('In this Adagio every-
thing must be played *piano* throughout. Only one *forte*
should occur. The piano solos should be as short and
expressive as possible. The tempo must be as slow as
possible'). Other fragments of works never completed include an early symphony in C (ff. 56-57b, 59, 71b, 127b-
128b, 158b-159b), earlier than the first symphony, op. 21;
fragments of this work occur in other sketchbooks described
by Nottebohm.

Of the first section of Add. MS. 29801 comprising the sketches, made in 1811, for the *Ruins of Athens* and *King Stephen* (ff. 1-37) little need be said here. Both works consisted of overtures and incidental music to plays by Kotzebue performed in celebration of the opening of the new theatre in Pest on 9 February 1812. Beethoven's music has only partially survived the absurdities of the pro-Austrian patriotic plots. In the *Ruins of Athens*, Minerva, accompanied by Mercury, is dismayed to find Athens in ruins and occupied by the Turks. But in Pest, the Muses are still honoured: 'Forget your Greece. It is past. The old one has vanished and a new one has come into being.' And Archduke Joseph, Prince Palatine of Hungary, is heralded as the leader of this revival.

The second in importance of the Museum sketchbooks is Add. MS. 31766 containing sketches for the Pastoral symphony, op. 68 (ff. 2-48b), the piano trios, op. 70, nos. 1 and 2 (ff. 39, 49-60b *passim*), and a definitive version of one passage in the 'cello sonata, op. 69 (f. 31b). The sketchbook was originally more extensive: the stubs of two leaves, clumsily cut out of the volume before it came to the Museum, are still visible. These have been identified by Dr Dagmar Weise, in the commentary accompanying her transcription of the Museum sketchbook, in Landsberg MS. 10 of the former Prussian State Library, Berlin, and in MS. Mh 74 of the Bodmer Collection now in the Beethoven House, Bonn. A further twenty-seven leaves, originally part of the London sketchbook, and also containing sketches for op. 68 and op. 70, have been identified by Dr Weise in the same Landsberg manuscript, which is a composite volume of sketches for 1805-23. It is not known who was responsible for the separation of the Landsberg leaves from the rest of the volume: it certainly took place before 1859, when the Landsberg Collection was acquired by the Prussian State Library in Berlin. It seems likely that the leaves were removed while, or shortly after, the sketches were in the possession of the family of the Karlsruhe Music Director, Ferdinand Simon Gassner, who died in 1851. Gassner had received all the sketches in 1842 as a gift from Anton Graeffer, a member of the publishing house of Artaria (according to the former's note on the inner cover of Add. MS. 31766). Graeffer possibly acquired the sketches at the sale of Beethoven's music on 5 November 1827. Of the later history of the London sketches, all that is known is that in 1876-77 they were in the possession of Adolf Horchler, court printer at Karlsruhe when Brahms tried to acquire them. The London volume subsequently appeared in a so-far unidentified English sale-catalogue. It was sold to the Museum by the collector Julian Marshall, with a large number of other music manuscripts, in a series of transactions between 10 July 1880 and 9 April 1881.

The series of sketches for the Pastoral symphony is the most comprehensive for any work of Beethoven preserved in the Museum. The transcription by Dr Weise makes clear the enormous detail and vast amount of repetition or near repetition in Beethoven's method of working at this stage. The sketches occur partly in the order of the five movements of the finished symphony, but some leaves, for example ff. 13b, 14, bear a bewildering medley of ideas for various movements. The sketches are exceptionally instructive in their indications of instrumentation, expression and phrasing. There are also references to the 'programme' of the work: f. 14 'donn[er]'; f. 33 'regen'; f. 29b 'Bliz'. Apart from these explicit notes, Beethoven told Schindler that the upward arpeggio on f. 9b, line 3, was intended to portray the song of the yellow-hammer. On the first page of the sketches (Plate III), Beethoven called the work 'Sinfonia caracteristica oder Erinnerungen an das Landleben' ('Characteristic symphony or reminiscences of country life') but he also added the more cryptic note: 'Man überlässt es dem Zuhörer sich selbst die Situationen auszufinden' ('Leave it to the listener to find out the situations for himself'). This caution in the face of too explicit a programme is expressed in another of Beethoven's notes on one of the Landsberg leaves: 'Jede Mahlerei nachdem sie in der Instrumentalmusik zu weit getrieben verliehrt' ('All painting loses something when it is taken too far in instrumental music').

The sketches in Add. MS. 31766 can be almost exactly dated. Beethoven has marked the first page '1808' and the work must have been completed by 11 September of that year, when Beethoven gave Breitkopf & Härtel a receipt for the payment of 100 ducats for five works, identifiable from the contract preserved in the Bodmer Collection, Beethoven House, Bonn, as symphonies 5 and 6, the piano trios, op. 70, no. 1 in D, with a second trio in an unspecified key, and the 'cello sonata, op. 69. It is obvious that once Beethoven had got past the sketching stage he worked at astonishing speed. In Add. MS. 31766 he indicated the instrumentation only summarily yet Breitkopf & Härtel presumably had a complete score in their possession by September. Beethoven's autograph full score is preserved in the Beethoven House; a copy corrected by him is in the University Library, Ljubljana.

A smaller miscellany (Add. MS. 29997) was purchased from Johann Nepomuk Kafka in 1876. This is only part of a larger group owned by Kafka: it contains several sketches for the late string quartet in C sharp minor, op. 131, and a haphazard collection of sketches for various works dating from 1799 to 1826. The sketches are very rough and some are still unidentified, but they include a possible sketch for the string quartet, op. 18, no. 4, fragments of the fourth and fifth piano concertos, part of *King Stephen*, some of Beethoven's settings of Scottish songs, and a discarded draft of the A minor quartet, op. 132.

The last of the Museum sketchbooks, Egerton MS. 2795, is a different kind of book. It was made by folding over eight

sheets of music paper and stitching them down the middle
to form a pocket-book of the type Beethoven used when
jotting down ideas out of doors. This example dates from
the summer of 1825, and contains sketches mainly for the
string quartet in B flat, op. 130. The sketches are brief and
written in pencil which 'makes them dismally hard to read'
according to Professor Kerman's recent study of the sketchbook. Fortunately two other sketchbooks of this time have
been preserved, the De Roda book, a sketchbook of eighty
pages, recently acquired by the Beethoven House, Bonn,
and another pocket-book in the Glinka Museum, Moscow,
and these facilitated Professor Kerman's elucidation of the
Egerton manuscript. Though mainly devoted to the B flat
quartet, Egerton MS. 2795 also contains scraps of other
works: on f. 4 is a sketch probably relating to the C sharp
minor quartet op. 131, and on f. 10 a draft canon on a text
from the Odyssey [xiv, 83, 84]: 'Alle gewaltsame That
misfällt ja den Göttern' ('All violent action displeases the
Gods'), a passage marked by Beethoven in his own copy of
Homer.

An isolated but very interesting sketch is Add. MS.
14396, f. 30, unique in the Museum as a sketch for one of
the late keyboard sonatas. Its identity was concealed by
the addition of bar-lines the whole height of the page,
which gave it the appearance of a full score. The sketches
are, in fact, jotted down in ordinary two-stave piano score,
as Beethoven has partly indicated at the side, and the
characteristic rhythm of the first movement of the Hammerklavier sonata, op. 106, dating from 1818, can be detected
on the recto. A few sketches headed '2tes Stük' are on the
verso. The leaf was formerly in the possession of Vincent
Novello who noted: 'Beethoven's hand-writing. Given to
me (on the very day that I had visited his Grave, July 27
1829) by Madame Streiker [Nanette Streicher], a Pupil
both of Mozart & Beethoven; & who was an old & sincere
friend of the latter great Composer.' Novello later noted

on 27 July 1843: 'I have the pleasure of presenting this rare and curious specimen of Beethoven's singular mode of making hasty memoranda and indicative sketches (which no one could understand but himself) of his Musical thoughts—for preservation in the Library of the British Museum.'

III

COMPLETE AUTOGRAPHS

Another interesting item, a complete autograph rather than a sketch, is Beethoven's cadenza, WoO 58b, for the third movement of Mozart's piano concerto in D minor, K. 466 (Add. MS. 29803, ff. 1-2b). The cadenza was probably written for performance by Ferdinand Ries, when he was in Vienna in 1802-05 or 1808-09. The cadenza for the first movement, which is preserved in the Beethoven House, Bonn, was formerly owned by Ries. The concerto was a favourite of Beethoven's, who performed it himself in 1795 and 1796, but this autograph cadenza is not likely to date from so early a period to judge from the handwriting. It was purchased by the Museum from Johann Nepomuk Kafka in 1875.

By far the most important of the complete autographs, as distinct from sketches, in the Museum, is Add. MS. 37767, a fair copy of the violin sonata in G, op. 30, no. 3. In this comparatively early work, dating from the beginning of 1802, Beethoven's hand is reasonably legible. The manuscript contains the complete work, though some passages of repetition are indicated by the note 'Come sopra'. Some corrections show the existence of earlier ideas: in the first movement more of the semiquaver passages were played in unison by the violin and piano, as in the first few bars; in the Tempo di Minuetto, the violin once had a version of the accompanying triplets of the left hand of the piano part (Plate IV) instead of slow, held chords. However, Beethoven's ultimate intentions, as printed in the first edition, *Trois sonates pour le pianoforte avec l'accompagnement*

13

d'un violon, Vienna, Bureau des arts et d'industrie, 1803, dedicated to Alexander I of Russia, are made clear. The manuscript (which bears the plate number '84' of this edition) was evidently sent to the publishers, and may have been used as the *Stichvorlage*, or copy from which the engraver worked.

The manuscripts of all three sonatas of op. 30 were apparently acquired by Tobias Haslinger at the auction of Beethoven's musical manuscripts held after his death, on 5 November 1827. Haslinger's son, Carl, presented the manuscript of the third sonata to the pianist Thérèse Wartel in 1843. It was later owned by Charles H. Chichele Plowden, whose daughter Harriet bequeathed it to the Museum in 1907.

Beethoven's relations with his friends, publishers and patrons were often stormy. Dissension was the background to one of the Beethoven autographs in the Museum, that of the song, the 'Lied aus der Ferne', WoO 137 (Add. MS. 47852, ff. 5-11), which came to the Museum in 1952 as part of the bequest of E. H. W. Meyerstein. This was one of seven settings of poems by Christian Ludwig Reissig, a German by birth who volunteered for the Austrian service in 1809, but received severe wounds in the fighting against Napoleon at Esslingen, near Vienna, the same year and was honourably discharged. Reissig's collection of poems, *Blümchen der Einsamkeit*, Vienna, 1809, enjoyed a considerable vogue and he requested, or perhaps commissioned (this is one of the disputed points), a number of composers, including Kozeluch, Salieri, Zelter, and many others as well as Beethoven, to make musical settings of them. He published a selection of these, including the 'Lied aus der Ferne' and three others by Beethoven, in *Achtzehn deutsche Gedichte*, Artaria, July 1810, which he dedicated to the Archduke Rudolph.

Beethoven's indignation at this publication was considerable, for he had already sent the manuscript of the song to Breitkopf & Härtel of Leipzig in August 1809. He wrote to Leipzig on 4 February 1810, asking them to hurry: 'The Gesang in der Ferne . . . is . . . written by a dilettante who urgently requested me to set his poem to music. But he has also taken the liberty of having the a[ria] engraved. So I thought that I would immediately give you a proof of my friendly feelings by informing you of this. I hope that as soon as you received it you gave it to be engraved. . . . If you make great haste, then the aria will arrive here before it can be published in Vienna.' Breitkopf & Härtel did, in fact, publish the song in February 1810, but do not seem to have informed Beethoven. On 15 October 1810, Beethoven was still urging them to publish: 'If you have not already done so, you ought now to publish at once the "Gesang aus der Ferne", which I once sent you. The poem is by that rascal Reissig.' On 11 October 1810, perhaps on receipt of an enquiry from Breitkopf & Härtel who also published two more of Beethoven's Reissig settings in op. 75 of October 1810 (although these had already been included in the Reissig publication), Beethoven had commented: 'It is an abominable lie that Captain Reissig ever paid me anything for my compositions. I composed those works for him as an act of friendship, because he was then a cripple. . . . I declare that Herren Breitkopf & Härtel are the sole owners.' Right might seem to be with Beethoven, but after his death the present manuscript was claimed by Artaria as their property and was awarded to them by the legal assessors. The pencilled name of Artaria on f. 5 of Add. MS. 47852 presumably dates from this assignment. A note of the Artaria publishing house on the title-page of a copy of the song in the Deutsche Staatsbibliothek, Berlin, which was used for their publication, claims that Beethoven sold this copy of the 'Lied aus der Ferne' to Reissig, who later sold his rights to Artaria.

The same volume (Add. MS. 47852) contains another Beethoven song, an autograph draft of 'Der Liebende',

WoO 139, also published by Reissig in *Achtzehn deutsche Gedichte*. Beethoven did not, apparently, protest about this publication. The first recto of the manuscript is marked by Beethoven in red crayon 'Skizzen'; it consists of a messy but legible draft of the song wanting only a few bars at the end. Like the other Reissig setting, 'Der Liebende' came to the Museum in 1952 as part of the Meyerstein Bequest.

IV

BEETHOVEN AND
GEORGE THOMSON

The remaining autograph music manuscript to be discussed is Egerton MS. 2327, dating from 1818, a curious memento of Beethoven's relations with George Thomson, a Scot (Plate V), whose enthusiasm for folksong led him to publish his collections. Thomson was employed for over fifty years as Secretary to the Board of Trustees for the Encouragement of Arts and Manufactures in Scotland, a post which allowed him sufficient leisure to undertake a vast correspondence and to travel in search of the folksongs of Scotland, Ireland and Wales. His published collections have several features which detract from their value to serious students of folksong: the melodies tend to be conflations of various sources, such texts as had survived were frequently not used by Thomson for his editions but were replaced by new words commissioned from a number of eminent writers, including Burns and Scott, and the accompaniments were likewise commissioned by Thomson from the first composers of the day, to his own requirements. He stipulated that preludes, ritornelli and codas should be written and that *ad lib.* parts should be provided for violin, flute and 'cello.

Thomson's correspondence with his writers and composers has been preserved, mainly in the British Museum, and consists of three large volumes of original letters to Thomson (Add. MSS. 35263-5) and four letterbooks covering the years 1803-51 (Add. MSS. 35266-9), in which Thomson kept copies of the letters he sent. The latter are not complete because none of the letters sent by Thomson to Beethoven before 1812 are recorded, although their existence is known from Beethoven's replies. Beethoven's first letter of 5 October 1803 acknowledges Thomson's proposal for some instrumental works: 'I am ready to compose for you six sonatas of the kind you wish, introducing in them Scottish airs in a manner which the Scottish nation will find the most acceptable and the most in accordance with the genius of its songs'. Like most of Beethoven's correspondence with Thomson, this letter was written by an assistant in French and signed by Beethoven; only a few of these letters are in the composer's hand. In subsequent letters Beethoven offered other works to Thomson—most of these were apparently never written, as it soon became evident that Thomson was not prepared to pay Beethoven's prices for works which did not relate to his passion for folksong, and he demurred considerably at Beethoven's terms for the folksong accompaniments. Thomson did go so far as to estimate the cost of publishing violin sonatas and string quintets by Beethoven. Two estimates in the Museum show that Thomson calculated in 1810 that he would need to sell 440 copies of the quintets at 15s. each, even to cover his costs, after he had paid Beethoven £40 for them (Plate VI); the second, undated but later, estimate is even more unfavourable: 850 copies at 15s. would be the necessary sale, allowing Beethoven £50.

It must soon have become as obvious to Thomson that negotiations would not proceed smoothly as it became clear to Beethoven that this was no great opportunity for the publication of his works. We can see Thomson trying to direct Beethoven into the production of facile works suitable for his limited market and Beethoven insisting that his work must be up to his own standards.

Thomson's first letter of 5 August 1812, preserved in the Museum letterbooks, acknowledges the receipt of Beethoven's accompaniments to fifty-three airs. After paying due compliments—'There is none which is not marked with the stamp of genius, science and taste'—he continues with a criticism, which was to become his constant complaint, of the difficulty of some of the accompaniments: 'In this country there is not one pianist in a hundred who can . . . play four notes in one hand and three in the other'. He asks Beethoven to rewrite two accompaniments and touch up some others and somewhat tactlessly refers to Haydn's amenability: 'Your great predecessor Haydn asked me to indicate frankly to him anything that did not please national taste in his ritornelli and accompaniments, and he willingly made changes'. Beethoven retorted on 19 February 1813: 'I am not accustomed to retouch my compositions. . . . It was your job to give me a better idea of the taste of your country and the lack of skill of your performers.' Thomson's continuing criticisms of undue difficulty led Beethoven to doubt whether the folksong commissions were worth his while, particularly as there was constant disagreement over prices: 'Were it not for a certain very particular regard and affection I feel for the English nation and also for Scottish melody, I would not undertake this task, neither for this fee nor for any other' he wrote on 15 September 1814.

Beethoven continually pressed Thomson to increase his payments. On 29 February 1812, he commented with some asperity (Plate VII): 'Haydn himself assured me that he also received four gold ducats for each song and he was writing only for piano and a violin without ritornelli and 'cello part. As for Monsieur Kozeluch, who supplies each song with an accompaniment for two ducats I congratulate you very much and also English and Scottish hearers if they enjoy them. I consider myself superior in this type of work to Monsieur Kozeluch (miserable creature). . . .' To which Thomson replied on 21 December 1812, when Beethoven's outburst had only just reached him, that Haydn had only asked two ducats but 'for the last twenty songs I gave him more at my own wish, because he had composed much for me really *con amore* and he had treated my suggestions with attention and politeness'. Thomson finally gave in and paid Beethoven four ducats a song on the understanding (15 October 1814) that Beethoven composed in his 'most simple, delicate and cantabile style'.

It has been calculated that Beethoven received not less than £550 for his 126 contributions to Thomson's publications; Haydn is said to have received £291 18s. for his accompaniments to 230 songs. Direct comparison is difficult owing to the devaluation of currency during the Napoleonic Wars, but it is certain that Beethoven drove a hard bargain. Thomson seems to have made little or nothing from Beethoven's settings; he complained on 22 June 1818: 'My songs with your ritornelli and accompaniments are not selling', and 'My enthusiasm for your compositions has caused me nothing but loss'.

Yet, whatever the musical merit of Beethoven's work for Thomson, and despite Thomson's complaints, it enjoyed considerable success in print. For, although the collections of Welsh and Irish songs were each printed only once, the Scottish ones proved exceptionally popular. Thomson laid the foundations in 1793, when he issued the first volume, with accompaniments by Pleyel. A second, with accompaniments by Kozeluch, followed in 1798. Haydn's work began in 1802, and the earlier volumes were reprinted, with changes and additions, until 1817 when the fourth volume appeared. It was in the fifth volume of 1818 that Beethoven's name appeared for the first time, with Haydn's alone. Then in 1822, all five volumes of Scottish songs were reprinted 'interspersed with those of Ireland and Wales', and the names of all four composers are given on the title-page. With further changes, additions and re-groupings, the Scottish songs were republished, in whole or part, in 1825, 1826, 1831, 1838, 1839 and 1841. Hummel made his first contribution in the twenty-five additional airs first printed in 1826, and Weber's work first appeared in a new edition of the whole collection issued in the same year. Such, in outline, is the story of Thomson's remarkable, protracted activity which lasted nearly half a century.

It produced many bibliographical puzzles which were solved for the first time by Cecil Hopkinson and the late C. B. Oldman in 'Thomson's Collections of National Song' (1940). They also showed that the number of surviving copies of most of the editions is few, and that the separate accompaniments for violin and violoncello are now very rare. Thomson lavished considerable pains and expense on both the octavo and the folio editions. He employed well-known artists to design very fine title-pages and elegant frontispieces, of a kind found in few of the continental editions of Beethoven's works. In the end, Beethoven provided accompaniments to 126 songs (41 Scottish, 59 Irish, 26 Welsh), a notable tribute to Thomson's pertinacity.

In 1816 Thomson approached Beethoven regarding another project arising from his interest in folksong. On 1 January, he asked Beethoven to send him specimens of other national airs, Russian, Spanish, Tyrolean, and so on. Thomson intended to commission English words to these but found this impossible, 'since the metre and singular style of these airs do not agree with the form and genius of English poetry'. Turning down Beethoven's suggestion that he should set prose, 'that is not our fashion', he proposed that Beethoven should compose pot-pourri overtures for the piano using these themes and material of his own. Beethoven delayed nearly a year before replying and then suggested a price too high for Thomson. Instead of abandoning the project, Thomson still attempted to turn it to account by a different suggestion on 25 June 1817: 'If you compose variations (not more than eight) for each air for the piano in an agreeable style, and not too difficult, I will pay you 72 ducats'. Beethoven's offer was for twelve

c

themes and variations for 100 ducats which Thomson accepted on 22 June 1818, only stipulating that there must be an *ad lib.* flute part as well. It is interesting that Thomson had remarked in a previous letter (28 December 1817): 'We have a large number of flautists but alas! our violinists are few, and very weak'. He reminded Beethoven once more: 'You must write the variations in a familiar, easy and slightly brilliant style; so that the greatest number of our ladies can play and enjoy them'. Beethoven set to work and the twelve themes noted in Egerton MS. 2327 were his record of the themes first sent to Thomson. The latter received the group with approval on 28 December 1818, but found, as usual, several points to criticise. Two were rejected outright as too difficult, and further objections followed. Thomson's eventual publication of July 1819 contained only six of the themes and variations originally submitted by Beethoven. As the Egerton manuscript contains only the themes and a few sketches of the variations, for an examination of the work we must turn to Thomson's edition, *Twelve National Airs with Variations for the Piano Forte and an accompaniment for the flute composed by Beethoven,* 1819, now very rare (Plate VIII). Despite this title-page, Thomson issued only nine themes and variations: six of those in the Egerton manuscript and three replacements sent by Beethoven. All Beethoven's variations, including those rejected by Thomson, were published within a year on the continent in Artaria's *Six thêmes variés bien faciles à éxécuter,* Vienna, September 1819, op. 105, which contained the variations already published by Thomson, and in Simrock's *Dix thêmes russes, ecossais et tyroliens variés pour le piano-forte avec accompagnement d'une flûte ou d'un violon,* Bonn and Cologne, August-September 1820, op. 107. The latter collection included seven themes and variations not published at all by Thomson, which was probably a breach of Beethoven's agreement with Thomson. However, the text of this contract has not survived. Thomson's last letter to Beethoven, of 14 June 1820, is an abortive attempt to obtain from him settings of six English airs in return for six themes and variations which Thomson had not used. He complains at the same time that the variations are not selling and that his outlay was a complete loss.

V

BEETHOVEN AND
ENGLISH PUBLISHERS

Beethoven's relations with other publishers cannot be so
well documented from sources in the Museum. A letter to
Robert Birchall of London, of 28 October 1815, announces
the despatch of the piano arrangement of the Battle symphony, on Wellington's victory at Vittoria. Beethoven asks
Birchall to make haste to engrave it and let him know the
date of publication. Birchall's publication appeared in
January 1816, thus antedating by a month the publication
by Steiner of Vienna. Beethoven had intended the publications to be simultaneous and was chagrined over Steiner's
delay. The symphony had been offered to Thomson in
October 1814, but Thomson had declined on 12 November,
in no uncertain terms: 'You ought to have explained your-
self more clearly; and you ought certainly to have fixed
your own price, as the vendor should do in all cases. You
are not aware, perhaps, that the score would not be of the
least use to me. In Great Britain we have so few persons
who play the violin well, that the sale of a symphony for full
orchestra would not meet the expense of engraving it. . . .
I should not print a symphony for full orchestra even
though you had made me a present of the score.' Beethoven
must have been disappointed, for several reasons, at the
English reception of this work, which he had intended as a
timely and possibly profitable tribute to the recent English
victories. Without going through the correct formalities of
asking in advance whether a dedication would be acceptable, he had sent a dedication copy of the work to the

Prince Regent in April 1814. Beethoven received neither the expected honorarium nor even an acknowledgement, but learnt from newspaper reports that it had been performed with great success at the Theatre Royal, Drury Lane, on 10 February 1815. Ten years later this still rankled. A draft letter of 1825 from Johann Andreas Stumpff, instrument-maker of London (Add. MS. 29260, f. 4), reports that Stumpff's enquiries made at Beethoven's request to members of the Royal Household had not met with any success, since nothing was known about the symphony and Sir Benjamin Bloomfield, who had been chief equerry to the Prince of Wales at the time, was now envoy to Sweden. Beethoven mentioned the matter to Sir George Smart when he met him the same year.

Beethoven's relations with Birchall are only one aspect of the publication of his music in England during his lifetime. It is not, perhaps, generally known that Beethoven's music became popular in England quite soon after the turn of the century. This may however seem less surprising if one remembers that the wide popularity of Haydn and Mozart had already opened the ears of the public to Viennese music. The evidence of the English taste for Beethoven was first assembled by Paul Hirsch (whose music library has already been mentioned) and C. B. Oldman, a specialist in this period, who was Principal Keeper of Printed Books in the British Museum from 1948 to 1959. Their investigation was published in 1953, under the title 'Contemporary English Editions of Beethoven', and revealed some remarkable facts.

Over 140 Beethoven works appeared, mostly in London, between 1799 and 1827. The works with opus number range from 1 to 127, with few omissions up to op. 97, and there were also published thirty-one compositions, mostly early, without opus number. As elsewhere, the earlier, less difficult ones were the most popular, no doubt because they were best suited to the limited resources of domestic performance. There were editions of over forty works for piano, a high proportion of which consisted of themes with variations.

Some thirty chamber works show how popular this type of music was. The other editions included concertos and symphonies (with a few notable exceptions issued in arrangements), songs, and some choral music. By far the most popular piece was the duet sonata, op. 6, which was printed by a dozen different publishers; next came the variations on 'Quant' è più bello', printed by ten. A good many other works were issued by four or five publishers. Well over forty firms found Beethoven profitable. The one with the largest Beethoven list was Monzani, who published at least seventy-five works of which, for convenient identification, he issued a thematic index. A similar index, but of fewer works, was issued by Preston. Such activity is clear evidence of demand. In about 1809, another prolific firm, Goulding & Co., copying Monzani, began to publish a *Selection of Beethoven's Piano Forte Music* which ultimately ran to at least thirty-two numbers.

Some of these English editions are of peculiar interest. The earliest of all is, indeed, unique. It is entitled *A Favourite Canzonetta, for the Piano Forte*, and was published in 1799 jointly by three firms, Broderip & Wilkinson, Hodsoll, and Astor & Co. The edition was entered at Stationers' Hall by William Wennington, a man of letters, who wrote the words, and who was in Vienna in the 1790s. Though some doubt may be cast on the authenticity of this work because nothing else is known about it, it provides early evidence of English interest in Beethoven. A different interest attaches to the scores of the Beethoven symphonies issued by Cianchettini & Sperati, a small but enterprising firm of Italian origin, as were so many of their more famous counterparts in Vienna. In May 1807, under the patronage of the Prince of Wales, they invited subscriptions for *A Compleat Collection of Haydn, Mozart and Beethoven's symphonies in score.* Two numbers appeared each month, the last probably in about the middle of 1809. The Beethoven symphonies were his first three, and this was their first publication in score, as it was also of the works by Haydn and Mozart. The Beethoven scores were, in fact, produced from the parts of the first editions which had been printed in Vienna shortly before. This Cianchettini edition was, therefore, pirated, and issued entirely without the composer's knowledge or approval. So, too, were the majority of the English editions published in his lifetime.

But there are some thirty editions which can be described as 'authentic', a term used to signify that they were in some degree published with Beethoven's knowledge and approval. Hirsch and Oldman realised that such editions were likely to be of considerable importance, but the pioneer nature of their work compelled them, as they wrote, 'to leave many points obscure', and consequently they could not attempt 'to investigate the textual reliability of any of these publications'. This task was undertaken by Dr Alan Tyson in his book *The Authentic English Editions of Beethoven*, 1963, to which this part of the present book is much indebted.

Six publishers were concerned, five in London and one in Edinburgh. The latter, George Thomson, had a protracted relationship with Beethoven, the important results of which have already been described in the context of the relevant manuscript documents. The London publishers were among the most distinguished of their day: they were Robert Birchall, Chappell & Co. with Goulding & Co., Muzio Clementi, Joseph Dale, and the Regent's Harmonic Institution. The relative quantity of their Beethoven publications can best be seen by listing them in summary tabular form:

Birchall	Sonata for violin and piano	Op. 47
	The Battle symphony, arranged for piano	Op. 91

Birchall (*continued*)	The seventh symphony, arranged for piano	Op. 92
	Sonata for violin and piano	Op. 96
	Piano trio	Op. 97
Chappell and Goulding	Piano trio	Op. 121a
Clementi	Piano sonata	Op. 31, no. 3
	Variations for piano on 'God Save the King'	WoO 78
	Three string quartets	Op. 59
	Violin concerto	Op. 61
	Violin concerto, arranged for piano	Op. 61
	Variations for piano	Op. 76
	Fantasia for piano	Op. 77
	Two sonatas for piano	Op. 78, 79
	'Remembrance' ('Andenken') Song	WoO 136
	Six songs	Op. 75
	String quartet	Op. 74
	Fantasia for piano and orchestra (parts)	Op. 80
	'Anxiety of Absence' ('Lied aus der Ferne') Song	WoO 137
	'The Lover' ('Der Liebende') Song	WoO 139
	Piano concerto	Op. 73
	Piano sonata, 'Les Adieux'	Op. 81a

Clementi (continued)	Five songs	Op. 82
	Piano sonata	Op. 110
	Piano sonata	Op. 111
	Bagatelles for piano	Op. 119
Dale	Bagatelles	Op. 33
Regent's Harmonic Institution	Piano sonata	Op. 106

Of the six firms in this list, only two, Birchall and Clementi, are known to have negotiated directly with Beethoven, and only Clementi (Plates IX, X) met him personally. The latter described this famous occasion in a vivid letter[1] which he wrote to his partner Collard:

Vienna, April 22nd, 1807.

Dear Collard: By a little management and without committing myself, I have at last made a complete conquest of the *haughty beauty*, Beethoven, who first began at public places to grin and coquet with me, which of course I took care not to discourage; then slid into familiar chat, till meeting him by chance one day in the street—'Where do you lodge?' says he; 'I have not seen you this *long* while!'—upon which I gave him my address. Two days after I find on my table his card, brought by himself, from the maid's description of his lovely form. This will do, thought I. Three days after that he calls again, and finds me at home. Conceive then the mutual ecstasy of such a meeting! I took pretty good care to improve it to *our house's* advantage, therefore, as soon as decency would allow, after praising very handsomely some of his compositions: 'Are you engaged with any publisher in London?'—'No' says he. 'Suppose then, that you prefer *me*?' —'With all my heart.' 'Done. What have you ready?' 'I'll bring you a list.' In short, I agreed with him to take in MSS. *three quartets*, a symphony, an *overture* and a *concerto for the violin*, which

[1] A facsimile of the autograph of the letter, as far as the words 'in proportion as you', was published in *The Athenaeum* for 26 July 1902, p. 135. The words printed in italic were underlined by Clementi.

is beautiful, and which, at my request, he will adapt for the pianoforte with and without additional keys; and *a concerto for the Pianoforte*, for *all* which we are to pay him two hundred pounds sterling. The property, however, is only for the British Dominions. To-day sets off a courier for London through Russia, and he will bring over to you 2 or 3 of the mentioned articles. Remember that the violin concerto he will adapt himself and send it as soon as he can. The quartets, *etc.*, you may get Cramer or some other very clever fellow to adapt for the P-forte. The Symphony and the Overture are wonderfully fine so that I think I have made a very good bargain. What do you think?— I have likewise engaged him to compose two sonatas and a fantasia for the Piano-forte which he is to deliver to our house for sixty pounds sterling (mind I have treated for Pounds, not Guineas). In short, he has promised to treat with no one but me for the British Dominions. In proportion as you receive his compositions you are to remit him the money. . . .

On account of the impediments by war, etc., I begged Beethoven to allow us 4 months (after the setting of his MSS.) to publish in. He said he would write to your house in French *stating the time*, for of course he sends them likewise to Paris, *etc.*, *etc.*, and they must appear on the same day . . . Mr. van Beethoven says, you may publish the 3 articles he sends by *this courier* on the 1st of September, next.

What Clementi ultimately achieved is shown in the long list of his editions on pp. 28-29. In the case of the other publishers, Beethoven acted through intermediaries. These included J. P. Salomon, a family friend from Bonn, Sir George Smart (see section VII), Charles Neate, whom Beethoven had met in Vienna in 1815, and his former pupil Ferdinand Ries.

In his study of the authentic editions, Dr Tyson has shown how much store Beethoven set by the publication of his music in England, and how complicated and, sometimes, how devious were his efforts to secure simultaneous publication in London and Vienna or Leipzig. He often conducted negotiations with two firms, one English, the other continental, at the same time, and sometimes in such a way that his bargain with the one should not be known to the other. He acted thus, largely for the sake of the double financial advantage. It was a matter of chance whether the English edition or the continental one appeared first. Moreover, as Dr Tyson has shown, such English editions derived from a different source; they therefore provide a text independent of the continental first editions, and their importance can hardly be overestimated.

The evidence for priority comes largely from the dated entries in the registers of Stationers' Hall in London, to which the law required the publisher to deliver eleven copies of each work. Stationers' Hall then passed one copy each to as many of the eleven privileged libraries as chose to exercise their right of demand. This is the principal source of the collections of the English Beethoven editions preserved in the British Museum, the Bodleian Library at Oxford, the University Library at Cambridge and in a few other libraries.

VI

ANNOTATED COPIES

Besides autograph manuscripts and correspondence there are in the Museum's collections a number of copies of works by Beethoven, both printed and manuscript, bearing annotations in his hand. One early item is Beethoven's own printed copy (Add. MS. 41631) of one of his first publications, the three early piano sonatas in E flat, F minor and D, WoO 47, published in 1783 under the imposing title, *Drei Sonaten fürs Klavier dem Hochwürdigsten Erzbischofe und Kurfürsten zu Köln Maximilian Friedrich meinem gnädigsten Herrn gewidmet und verfertiget von Ludwig van Beethoven alt eilf Jahr* (Speier, In Rath Bosslers Verlage). The statement that Beethoven was only eleven derives from his family's claim that he was born in 1772. The Elector of Cologne, to whom the sonatas are dedicated, was Beethoven's first patron. It has been suggested that the humble dedication may have been drafted for Beethoven by his teacher, Christian Gottlob Neefe; the style is poetic, rhetorical and strangely at variance with Beethoven's later manner of expression and obstinate independence of behaviour: 'I have now reached my eleventh year; and since then my Muse has often whispered to me in hours of inspiration: Make an attempt. Write down the harmonies of your soul! Eleven years, I thought, and how would I look as a composer? And what would men of art have to say to it? I was rather shy. But my Muse would have it—I obeyed—and wrote.' An autograph note of Beethoven's added at the side of the title-page (Plate XI) at a much later date, to judge from the handwriting, reads: 'Noch vor diesem Werke sind

Variationen in C moll wie auch Lieder in einem Bossleri-
schen Jornal erschienen' ('Variations in C minor and songs
in a Bossler journal appeared before this work'), a reference
to the nine variations in C minor on a march of E. C.
Dressler, WoO 63, published in 1782, and to two songs,
WoO 107, 108, included by Bossler in his weekly musical
publication, *Blumenlese für Klavierliebhaber*, 1783-84.

This copy of Beethoven's early sonatas was formerly
owned by the Mozart scholar, Professor Otto Jahn of Bonn;
in 1870, it came into the possession of the pianist Johann
Ernst Perabo, who died in 1920, and it was presented by
his pupil, Edward Perry Warren, to the Museum in 1928,
together with important music manuscripts from the Perabo
collection, including a copy of the piano solo part of the
triple concerto, op. 56, with autograph annotations by
Beethoven (Add. MS. 41630, ff. 1-41).

This piano part is of particular interest, as it was the
Stichvorlage for the first edition, in parts, by the Bureau des
arts et d'industrie, Vienna, June-July 1807, and bears the
plate number '519' of this edition on the title-page. For his
earlier works, Beethoven seems to have sent autograph
copies to the publishers. Later, he said in a letter to
Breitkopf & Härtel of 2 November 1809: 'It is impossible
always to send copies in my own handwriting', but he goes
on to say that he had checked and corrected the copyists'
work. The publishers may have been grateful to be spared
the task of deciphering Beethoven's handwriting, but
Beethoven's corrections were not always as thorough as they
should have been. However, one divergence between the
manuscript piano part and the first edition, two extra bars
of chromatic scale in the cadenza of the third movement
(before bar 435 of the Eulenburg score), was the subject
of subsequent revision by Beethoven. A copy in full score
of this movement, with autograph corrections by Beethoven
(now preserved in the Deutsche Staatsbibliothek, Berlin,
Beethoven Autograph MS. Artaria 155), also contains these

two bars, but they are here crossed through. The piano part, formerly in the possession of Carl Haslinger, appeared in a sale-catalogue of List & Francke, Leipzig, 12 June 1882, lot 5, and was subsequently owned by Perabo.

It has already been seen that Clementi asked Beethoven to prepare a version of the violin concerto for piano and orchestra, a fact which probably was not widely known in England until John Ogden revived the piano version at a Festival Hall concert on 20 February 1969. Both versions of the concerto, op. 61, were first published in Vienna by the Bureau des arts et d'industrie in August 1808, while Clementi's editions, again of both versions, did not appear until the autumn of 1810. The source of the Vienna edition was not the autograph manuscript of the concerto preserved in the National Library at Vienna, which is an early source for the work confirming Czerny's statement that Beethoven composed it in a great hurry: several alternative versions of the solo part are given and in places all of them disagree with the Vienna edition. Rather, it has recently been proved by Dr Alan Tyson that a manuscript copy of the full score giving both the violin and piano solo parts preserved in the Museum since 1952, when it was received as part of the Meyerstein Bequest, is the *Stichvorlage* of both Vienna editions.

Although the manuscript (Add. MS. 47851) is in a copyist's hand, there are numerous annotations and corrections by Beethoven in pencil, ink and his characteristic red crayon, showing that he checked the manuscript, none too efficiently, before it went to the publishers. The manuscript is important, not so much as a source for the concerto, but as evidence showing how corruptions crept into the text at an early stage. Ambiguities in this manuscript led to such gross errors in the Vienna edition as the direction 'sempre fortissimo' in the piano solo part at bar 301 of the first movement where the piano part in the Meyerstein manuscript has 'espressivo', not very clearly written. Another error arising from this manuscript is the omission in the Vienna edition and many subsequent ones of the 'cello thematic line in the Coda of the first movement. The Meyerstein manuscript is not clear at this point, as it omits the first three bars of the 'cello part, at bars 525-7, although the continuation is given (Plate XII), so that the engraver started to engrave the 'cello part the same as the bass, as was the convention elsewhere in this manuscript where no separate part is given, and continued to do so even where there was a separate line in the score. Beethoven did not notice this ambiguity when he checked the copy. The complete 'cello part is given in the Vienna autograph and has been incorporated into some modern editions.

It is now known that Clementi's source was a manuscript set of orchestral parts copied from the autograph in 1807. He is correct in some places where the Meyerstein manuscript is inaccurate or misleading, but he also omits the 'cello line in the Coda. Some of Clementi's readings are those of the much earlier Vienna autograph, but variants in his violin solo part, which is made to conform to the piano version in places, are not corroborated by the Vienna manuscript.

Having served its purpose as a *Stichvorlage*, Add. MS. 47851 was presented by Beethoven to Charles Neate in 1816 and remained in the possession of the latter's family until 1911. Neate, a pianist, 'cellist and composer, and a founder-member of the Philharmonic Society, was in Vienna from May 1815 to February 1816. He saw Beethoven frequently and as well as purchasing three overtures for the Philharmonic Society, he was entrusted by Beethoven with copies of several of his works, including the seventh symphony, op. 92, the string quartet, op. 95, and the 'cello sonatas, op. 102, with a view to finding an English publisher for them. The *Stichvorlage* of the violin concerto seems to have been given to him as a parting present: 'La Partition du Concert pour le Violon vous ne

refuserès comme sovenir de moi', runs a note of Beethoven
of *c.* 6 February 1816. As it happened, on his return to
England Neate became distracted, partly by the difficult
circumstances attending his marriage, and was not successful in placing any of the Beethoven works with English
publishers. He was pursued by a series of recriminations
from the impatient and suspicious composer: 'I swear that
you have done nothing for me and that you will do nothing and
again *nothing* for me, summa summarum, *nothing! nothing!
nothing!!!*' (19 April 1817). It is to Neate's credit that he
was not so mortified as to break off relations with Beethoven
completely. He continued to correspond with him at
intervals and in 1824 was entrusted with further negotiations with Beethoven on behalf of the Philharmonic Society.
In 1827, when the news of Beethoven's serious illness
reached London, it was Neate who proposed the advance
of £100 from the Society to Beethoven.

VII

THE MOUNT OF OLIVES

An interesting manuscript with numerous revisions is a copy with autograph corrections by Beethoven of the score of his only completed oratorio, *Christus am Oelberge* usually known in England as *The Mount of Olives*, op. 85 (Egerton MS. 2727). The history of this work is complicated. Beethoven wrote it in a great hurry in 1803, just before its first performance at the Theater an der Wien on 5 April. This was successful and other performances followed that year. Before sending it to Breitkopf & Härtel for publication on 26 August 1804, Beethoven revised it: 'I have added an entirely new chorus and have also made a few alterations, the reason being that I wrote the whole work in a few weeks and that naturally some passages did not altogether satisfy me later on'. Negotiations for publication dragged on for years, and the work was not printed until October 1811. Not all the source materials for this work have survived; from references to it in his letters, Beethoven seems to have made further revisions both to the music and the text. On 23 August 1811, when he was revising the proofs, he wrote to Breitkopf & Härtel: 'I had just started to revise the oratorio. . . . Here and there the text must remain in its original form. I know that the text is extremely bad.' In the Egerton manuscript which seems to have been the *Stichvorlage* for the Breitkopf edition, for Beethoven's numerous corrections are faithfully reflected in the Breitkopf score, there are two texts entered throughout, the original being in brown ink and a later one in red. Occasionally there is even a third text. An employee of Breitkopf

& Härtel has indicated, presumably on Beethoven's instructions, which text is to appear in the edition. In one instance at least these instructions were misinterpreted. Beethoven complains in a letter to Breitkopf of 28 January 1812: 'In spite of my note in favour of the old text in the oratorio chorus "Wir haben Ihn gesehen" you have again retained the *unfortunate* alteration'. But the Breitkopf edition follows the directions given in the Egerton manuscript at this point (f. 95b) to use the red text. Another source for the oratorio, a score also revised by Beethoven but not so completely as the Egerton manuscript, is preserved in the Deutsche Staatsbibliothek, Berlin.

The Egerton manuscript was purchased in 1889 from Emanuel Nowotny of Graz, who bought it after the death of Julius Rietz (1812-77), court music director at Dresden. Rietz had previously held several leading musical positions in Leipzig where he presumably acquired the manuscript from the archives of Breitkopf & Härtel.

VIII

BEETHOVEN AND
SIR GEORGE SMART

The Mount of Olives appears to have enjoyed considerable popularity in England during the first part of the nineteenth century, judging from the number of early English editions and arrangements of the work. The first English performance was on 25 February 1814, at the Theatre Royal, Drury Lane, and was due to the initiative of Sir George Smart (Plate XIII) who introduced it in the second season of Lenten oratorios which he conducted in London from 1813 to 1825. In his memoranda books preserved in the Museum (Add MS. 41772, 42225, etc.) he noted that the oratorio was performed ten times during the twelve nights of this season and that it was also given in Liverpool on 10 May. Smart was so enthusiastic about the work that he published his own piano arrangement through Chappell in 1814 to an English adaptation of the text by S. J. Arnold. A note in this edition made it clear that the English version was no mere translation: 'The Author has thought it proper to alter the *Persons*, in conformity to the national feelings of religious propriety, which would be justly outraged by introducing the Saviour of the World as a character of the Drama'. Instead of Christus, Arnold's version gave a 'Tenor voice'. Although Smart's arrangement presumably appeared without any prior agreement with Beethoven, the extant correspondence between Beethoven and Smart, which opens in 1815, is couched in amicable terms and there is no hint that Beethoven felt any sense of grievance. Beethoven seems to have regarded Smart

39

as a person of influence and integrity, to whom he could turn in his many difficulties connected with the English market for his publications. Smart was an extremely able and versatile man; a composer himself, with considerable knowledge of singing and some skill on the organ and violin, he was also active as a conductor and impresario. He was extremely influential in English musical life up to his death in 1867, and the summaries of the concerts and music festivals with which he was connected, preserved in his memoranda books now in the Museum, make impressive reading. It is hardly surprising that Beethoven turned to Smart when he thought that Neate was procrastinating or deceiving him over the works entrusted to him for sale in England. Here it is obvious that Smart smoothed over the difficulties. Smart's introduction of the Battle symphony to England, on 10 February 1815, oddly enough in his third season of Lenten oratorios, might have been a cause of dissension with Beethoven, who knew that the source for the performance was the copy of the score sent to the Prince Regent, which had not been acknowledged in any way. So far as Smart was concerned, Beethoven thanked him for his interest in promoting the work and enquired about the prospects of publishing it in England.

As one of the regular conductors for the Philharmonic Society, it fell to Smart to conduct the first performance in England of the ninth symphony, which took place on 21 March 1825, after a surprisingly short period of preparation. The performance, Smart recorded, took one hour four minutes (Add. MS. 41779, f. 11b). In July the same year, Smart left for Germany and he noted that 'his principal reason for this journey was, to ascertain from Beethoven personally the exact times of the Movements in his *Characteristic* [i.e. the ninth] and of some of his other Sinfonias'. It was Smart's habit to keep records of timings for many of the works which he conducted during the course of his long career. He noted the details on many of the concert programmes, which he collected assiduously. (A large collection of them was bequeathed to the British Museum and is now preserved in the Department of Printed Books.) Smart's practice in conducting was rather inconsistent, so that it is hard to say at which performances he made cuts or omitted repeats. Though his timings for the same work naturally varied at different periods of his career, he tended generally to take most music rather slower than is usual today. As is mentioned on p. 42, Smart thought the time suggested by Beethoven himself for the ninth symphony was impossibly fast. Valuable as is the evidence from Smart's timings, it is rather contradictory. It has been analysed, both for Beethoven and other composers, in an article by Dr Nicholas Temperley. Smart kept a journal of his 1825 tour (Add. MSS. 41774, 41771) in which he records that his first meeting with Beethoven was on 9 September, at the Hotel Wilden Mann (that is the inn 'Zum wilden Mann') in Vienna, the lodging of Moritz Schlesinger, the Paris music publisher. Beethoven had come in from Baden, the spa near Vienna, where he was in the habit of passing the summer, for a trial of his new string quartet in A minor, op. 132, which Schlesinger was considering for publication. The quartet was performed twice before 'a numerous assembly of Professors' by Schuppanzigh, Holz, Weiss and Linke under Beethoven's direction. Smart noted: 'a staccato passage not being expressed to the satisfaction of his *eye* for alas! he could not *hear*—he seized hold of Holtz's Violin and played the passage about a quarter of a tone too flat'. Smart was received 'in the most flattering manner' by Beethoven and was invited to Baden on the Sunday following. This visit being postponed, as Beethoven came to Schlesinger's again, Smart was once more welcome at the Hotel Wilden Mann to hear the quartet played again by the same performers, and one of the piano trios, op. 70, in which Czerny joined. At dinner after the rehearsal, Smart surprised Beethoven by showing him a poster of an

English concert when *The Mount of Olives* and the Battle symphony were given on the same evening. They had been performed together on seven occasions between 1815 and 1820 at the Theatre Royal, Drury Lane, after Smart's introduction of the symphony in February 1815. After dinner, Beethoven was asked to improvise on a theme suggested by Smart: 'He did so for 20 minutes, in a most extraordinary manner—sometimes very Fortissimo—but full of genious—he was greatly agitated at the conclusion of his playing'.

On Friday, 16 September, Smart paid his postponed visit to Beethoven at Baden and took the opportunity to enquire about the ninth symphony: 'Beethoven gave me the time, by playing the subjects on the P.F. of many movements in his Sinfonie &c. including the Choral Sinfonia, which according to *his* Account took ¾ of an hour only in performance, *we* know that is impossible—at Vienna the Recit was played by 4 Celli & 2 Contra Bassi which certainly is better than having the Tutti Bassi'. Smart notes that he had 'a long conversation on musical subjects' with Beethoven 'during which he expressed his great desire to come to England'. They then took a walk together before dinner, 'Beethoven generally in advance humming some passage, he usually sketches his subjects in the open air. . . '. Unfortunately Smart did not write down all their conversation in his journal. On departing, he gave Beethoven his diamond pin and Beethoven 'wrote me the following Canon as fast as his Pen would write in about 2 minutes of time as I stood at the Door ready to depart'. A facsimile of the canon, 'Ars longa, vita brevis', appears in Cox's edition of Smart's journal.

IX

BEETHOVEN AND
THE PHILHARMONIC SOCIETY

The ninth symphony is only the best-known aspect of the
relations of the Philharmonic Society with Beethoven.
Other details can be found in the archives of the Society
on loan to the Museum. The Society had performed a
Beethoven symphony at their first concert on 8 March
1813, and they gave the *Eroica* on 28 February 1814. In
1815, negotiations were opened with Beethoven to secure
new works for performance by the Society, through the
intermediacy of Charles Neate, who, as we have seen, was
then on a visit to Vienna. At a general meeting on 11 July
1815, the directors of the Society were requested to pur-
chase from Beethoven, for 75 guineas, three overtures 'for
the Society'. Reading between the lines of the extant
evidence, it seems that the Society was disappointed in the
three overtures sent by Beethoven through Neate in return
for this fee. They proved to be the overtures *The Ruins of
Athens*, op. 113, *King Stephen*, op. 117, and *Namensfeier*,
op. 115. Only the last of these was new: the first two were
written with incidental music to two plays by Kotzebue,
performed at the opening of the new theatre in Pest on
9 February 1812. Even op. 115 was first performed in
Vienna on 25 December 1815, although the Philharmonic
Society do not appear to have known of this performance:
they included an overture in C, probably op. 115, at a
public concert on 25 March 1816, the programme stating
inaccurately: 'manuscript composed for the Society and
never before performed'. The other two overtures were not

43

performed at early Philharmonic Society concerts, although they must have been played through at trial nights, as was the custom with new works, and subsequently rejected. Reports of the lack of success of these performances reached Beethoven through Neate. On 18 December 1816, Beethoven replied: 'I was very sorry to hear that the three Overtures were not liked in London. I by no means reckon them amongst my best works (which however I may boldly say of the Symphony in A), but still they were not disliked here. . . . Was there no fault in the execution?' Beethoven appears on the defensive on the same subject in a letter to Smart of October 1816: 'Mr Neate had in his possession other more essential works, he chose those three and it is very unfortunate that on account of them according to his judgment my musical name is all at once sunk to nothing . . .'—which is unfair to Neate. The Society did show interest in the symphony in A, no. 7, op. 92, for a directors' minute of 12 January 1817 asked Neate 'to write the order for the New Sym[phony] of Beethoven in A'. However, Beethoven had already sold the work to Steiner of Vienna who published it in November 1816.

In the summer of 1817, the Philharmonic Society was ready to negotiate with Beethoven again. Through Ferdinand Ries, Beethoven's pupil, now resident in London, and an influential member of the Society, Beethoven was invited to visit London in January 1818 'writing two New Symphonies to remain the property of the Society' for the fee of 300 guineas. Beethoven's reaction to this proposal was to ask for a further 100 guineas for travelling expenses and 150 in advance. At this, the Philharmonic Society remained firm, and a directors' meeting on 19 August 1817 instructed Ries to repeat their original offer. The following spring Beethoven raised the matter again, with no mention of terms: his health was too bad at present, but he hoped to be available later in the year. The visit did not take place.

In a letter to Ries of 6 July 1822, Beethoven enquired:

'Have you any idea what fee the *Harmony Society* would offer me for a grand symphony?'. Emily Anderson suggested that this was the first extant mention of the ninth symphony. On 10 November 1822, a directors' meeting resolved that 'an offer of £50 be made to Beethoven for a M.S. Sym^y. He having permission to dispose of it at the expiration of Eighteen Months after the receipt of it. It being a proviso that it shall arrive during the Month of March next.' Beethoven accepted the offer in a letter to Ries of 20 December 1822, 'Even though the fee to be paid by the English cannot be compared with the fees paid by other nations'! Early in 1823, Beethoven sent, as 'proof of my affection', another overture to the Society, *Die Weihe des Hauses*, op. 124, composed for the opening of the Josephstadt Theater in Vienna and performed there on 3 October 1822. This was well received and the Society authorised the payment of £25 to Beethoven at their meeting on 25 January 1823 (a surprisingly high figure when they were offering only £50 for a symphony), and performed the overture at their concert on 21 April the same year. Regarding the symphony, Beethoven was dilatory. On 5 February, he wrote to Ries: 'If I were not so poor as to have to live by my pen, I would not accept anything from the P[hilharmonic] Soc[iety]. As things are, however, I am obliged to wait until the fee for the symphony has been forwarded to Vienna . . . the Society may keep it [i.e. the overture] and the symphony too for 18 months. For I would only publish it after that time.' Beethoven is prevaricating by suggesting that the symphony was ready. In July 1823, writing to the Archduke Rudolf to explain his delay in finishing the Missa Solemnis, he says he hoped to finish the symphony 'in less than a fortnight'. According to Schindler, the score was not ready until February 1824, and there is evidence in Beethoven's correspondence that the copying of parts and several scores was in progress in April. Meanwhile the Philharmonic Society was getting

impatient, and Ries was asked at a directors' meeting of
4 January 1824 'to write to Vienna to know when
Beethoven's Symphony is likely to arrive and pressing for
its being forwarded without delay'. On 27 April 1824, Franz
Christian Kirchhoffer of Vienna, who acted as intermediary
in the transmission of the Society's copy to London, finally
obtained a receipt from Beethoven (Add. MS. 33965, f. 174)
for the £50 'for my symphony delivered to him [Kirch-
hoffer] which I have composed for the Philharmonic Society
in London'. The score did not arrive in London until
December, when Neate wrote to acknowledge its receipt.

The score of the ninth symphony sent to the Society bears
a note in Beethoven's hand stating once more that it was
'written for the Philharmonic Society in London'. Yet it
was first performed at a benefit concert for Beethoven in
Vienna at the Kärnthnerthor Theater on 7 May 1824, and
repeated there on 23 May, and was published in Germany,
by Schott of Mainz, in August 1826, with a dedication to
Friedrich Wilhelm III, King of Prussia. It seems, however,
that Beethoven acted strictly within the terms of his agreement with the Society. He confirmed in letters to Neate and
Ries of January and February 1825 that the time limit
for publication would be respected, and discounted rumours
that the work had been sent to Paris and Bremen as well
as to Schotts at Mainz. To Neate he gave some hints on
rehearsal: 'You must have limited rehearsals, perhaps four
parts at a time; for this is the only way to study such a work
well; above all the choruses must be well practised'. He
mentioned that there were still some errors in the score.

The last contact between Beethoven and the Philharmonic Society was in sadder circumstances. On 8 February
1827, when desperately ill with dropsy, Beethoven wrote to
Johann Andreas Stumpff, the instrument-maker of London,
thanking him for his gift of the Arnold edition of Handel,
which Stumpff had sent, care of Johann Baptist Streicher
of Vienna, for transmission to 'the greatest living composer,

as a sign of the greatest esteem'. Beethoven describes this as 'a royal gift'. He asked Stumpff to remind the Society of their proposal a few years previously to hold a benefit concert for him in London. Similar appeals went to Smart and Moscheles, mentioning his failing health and indifferent circumstances. The Society responded at their genera meeting on 28 February by sending £100 through Moscheles, in advance of a concert, 'to be applied to his comforts and necessities during his illness'. Beethoven was greatly moved by this generosity, and in his letter of thanks addressed to Moscheles for transmission to the Society dictated to Schindler on 18 March 1827, only eight days before his death, he said: 'I will undertake to return to the Society my warmest thanks by engaging to compose for it either a new symphony, sketches for which are already in my desk, or a new overture, or something else which the Society might like to have'. This was the projected tenth symphony, which might therefore have come to the Philharmonic Society had Beethoven lived. Schindler said in a letter to Moscheles, published by the latter in his translation of Schindler's biography of Beethoven, that Beethoven 'would have his sketch of the Tenth Symphony brought to him, concerning the plan of which he talked to me a great deal. It was destined for the Philharmonic Society, and according to the form which it assumed in his morbid imagination, it was to be a musical leviathan, compared with which his other Grand Symphonies would be merely trifling performances.' In a letter to Smart of 2 April 1827, after Beethoven's death, Schindler said: 'We shall not neglect, if amongst the property, only one complete unknown work should be found, to transmit the same to the Society, as a Souvenir of the deceased'. The generosity of the Society extended after Beethoven's death: the £100 was found intact among Beethoven's effects but after suitable enquiry, learning of Beethoven's anxiety for his nephew and ward, Karl, the Society decided, at Moscheles's suggestion, not to reclaim it, but to allow it to pass to Beethoven's estate.

Some relics of Beethoven's death passed to the Philharmonic Society by chance, at a later date. These include a lock of his hair which was cut off an hour after his death, according to notes preserved with it. Gerhard von Breuning stated that all Beethoven's hair was cut off shortly after his death by 'unknown hands'. Half a laurel leaf from one of the three wreaths thrown by Hummel onto Beethoven's grave and an invitation card to his funeral were formerly in the possession of Beethoven's friend, Paul Friedrich Walther.

X

THE NINTH SYMPHONY

In the collection of music manuscripts belonging to the Philharmonic Society on loan to the Museum are still preserved the copies of the works sent by Beethoven consisting of the three overtures, op. 113, op. 115 and op. 117, sent in 1815, the later overture, op. 124, sent in 1823, and, most important, the copy of the score of the ninth symphony, op. 125. The three earlier overtures and the beginning and end of op. 124 are the work of Beethoven's regular copyist, Schlemmer; all have autograph inscriptions on the title-pages by Beethoven. The copy of op. 115 also has a number of autograph corrections by Beethoven originally written in pencil but inked over by a different hand.

The full score of the ninth symphony (RPS. 21) bears Beethoven's autograph inscription on the title-page: 'Grosse Sinfonie geschrieben für die philarmonische Gesellschaft in London'. Apart from the headings to the movements only very few of the numerous corrections and additions to the manuscript may be in Beethoven's hand. Most of the corrections refer to omitted dynamics and clefs or to other obscurities in the score. A number of annotations were obviously made by the conductors of early performances in England and draw attention to unusual features of the work, particularly in the last movement. They include on f. 96 a conductor's memorandum to bear in mind the semiquaver passage at the end of the section and not to set too fast a tempo (Plate XIV). In the first movement at bar 217 (f. 17), RPS. 21 shows evidence of a change of plan in Beethoven's harmony: some of the string parts are in F minor, others in C minor; the autograph score (see the facsimile of the autograph manuscript in Berlin, published in Leipzig, 1924) also shows a mixture of harmonies at this point, although Beethoven has altered the oboe part to C minor and there seems no reason to doubt that this was his final intention. Moscheles's marginal note in RPS. 21, altering the oboe part back to F minor, cannot have helped, as he did not alter the conflicting string parts. Beethoven's copyist, Wenzel Schlemmer, had died on 6 August 1823, and Beethoven frequently referred in his letters after this date to the difficulties he had in getting works copied accurately. As many as five different copyists were employed on the copy of the ninth symphony sent to Schotts, and there are two main hands in the RPS. 21; one as far as f. 147, while the second completes the last movement at ff. 148-62. The copyists of the Philharmonic Society's score have not yet been identified. Other copies of the score were made for the King of Prussia (the dedication copy is now in Berlin) and for Ries's performance at the Lower Rhine Festival of 1825 (now at Aachen). The parts used for the first performance in Vienna are preserved there in the library of the Gesellschaft der Musik-freunde. No complete study of all aspects of this wealth of materials has been published.

XI

ENGLISH PERFORMANCES
OF BEETHOVEN

So far as the first public performance in England of the
ninth symphony is concerned, one can only be astonished
that it was put on at such short notice. From Smart's letters
to the Philharmonic Society it is obvious that he was not
happy about the situation, particularly as there was some
prospect of Beethoven's coming to London. Negotiations
had been opened once more, but Beethoven's terms again
caused the visit to fall through. On 30 January 1825, the
Directors instructed Neate to write to Beethoven saying that
the Society was 'willing to abide by its first offer' (that is,
300 guineas). Smart wrote to the Society on 12 March: 'In
my humble opinion it will be better to postpone the performance of Beethoven's new Sinfonia till his definite
answer is received, for should he decide upon coming during the Season, will it be judicious to perform it without
him . . . for I have not the vanity to imagine that I can fully
enter into the ideas of the Composer and, I candidly own,
that I do not understand his meaning as to the style of the
Recitative for the Basses, perhaps it should be play'd faster'.
A trial of the symphony had already taken place under
Smart's direction on 1 February, so that he was fully aware
of the hazards of the work. This rehearsal was held at very
short notice, for the Directors resolved on 2 January that
it should take place 'provided it [i.e. the parts] can [be]
finished Copying'. Critics of the trial in *The Quarterly Musical
Magazine* and *The Harmonicon* confined their attention
mainly to the difficulties of the work rather than the

imperfections of the performance: William Ayrton of *The Harmonicon* considered that 'it manifests many brilliant traits of Beethoven's vast genius . . .' but that it was much too long and was 'rendered wearying by expansion'. Their reactions to Smart's first public performance were similar: 'at least twice as long as it should be' (*The Harmonicon*).

The soloists at the first London performance at the Argyll Rooms, on 21 March 1825, were Mme Caradori, Miss Goodall, Mr Vaughan and Mr Phillips. In the last movement the instrumental recitatives appear to have been played as solos by Dragonetti, the famous double-bass virtuoso. He wrote to the Society on 21 January 1825: 'I will accept the engagement for the ensuing Season at 10 Guineas per night, and play all the Solo's [*sic*] in Beethoven's new Symphony . . . I beg to leave to add, that I saw the score of Beethoven last Sunday, and had I seen it before I sent in my terms I would have asked double'. Dragonetti continued to play the recitatives as a solo until his death in 1846.

Smart, who had the score, superintended the performance from the piano, but the main burden of maintaining the ensemble must have rested with Franz Cramer, the leading violin. There is no evidence that a visible time-beat was given at the first two London performances, although this was the custom in Vienna. Spohr's method of conducting with a baton, which he had tried out on the Philharmonic Society in 1820, was not accepted by the Society until the 1830s, despite his optimistic remark in his autobiography that no one ever conducted from the piano again at a Philharmonic concert.

Fortunately, Smart was able to carry out his wish to conduct a further performance after his visit to Beethoven. He was disappointed in 1828: in a letter to the Society he happily accepted an invitation to direct a trial performance on 31 January, mentioning that 'I have had a long conversation with Beethoven relative to this Sym^y. And I should like the effects to be produced as he pointed out as far as I have the power', but the idea was dropped, perhaps because Smart insisted that he would need the whole evening for the trial. On 26 April 1830, he did conduct the symphony once more at Neate's benefit concert at the King's Theatre Concert Room. According to *The Harmonicon* 'it was executed admirably, and seemed to afford the audience much satisfaction. We certainly do not at present rank ourselves among its admirers, and moreover cannot suppose that we shall ever enjoy a work in which there are so many extravagances, which is of so heterogeneous a nature, and is an hour and a quarter in duration.'

Criticisms of other major works of Beethoven when first performed in London, read strangely now. After its first performance by Eliason at a Philharmonic Society concert on 9 April 1832, the violin concerto was thus dismissed by *The Harmonicon*: 'it is a *fiddling* affair, and might have been written by any third or fourth-rate composer'. It was not until the youthful Joachim, aged thirteen, performed it at a Philharmonic concert on 27 May 1844, with Mendelssohn as conductor, that it was appreciated in London.

Fidelio, on the other hand, was well received at its first complete performance in London, at the King's Theatre on 18 May 1832. Even the fastidious critic of *The Harmonicon* wrote: 'Let then all true lovers of music hear "Fidelio". Should they think as we do, that its defect is sameness and want of relief—should they even feel the last note as a welcome sound—still they will have heard enough to amply recompense them for whatlike trouble and expense they may have incurred.'

A number of other early performances of works by Beethoven were given at private concerts in London. Prominent among these were the musical gatherings held by Thomas Alsager of *The Times*, at his residence in Queen Square. Alsager was described by Moscheles as 'a complete

E

fanatic in his Beethoven worship. In his large music room Beethoven's works were given with full orchestral accompaniments.' On 24 December 1832, Moscheles was asked to conduct there Beethoven's Mass in D, op. 123, 'a work hitherto unknown and unheard in London'. Moscheles wrote in his diary: 'I had become by dint of study completely absorbed in that colossal work (the Messe Solennelle). Occasionally isolated phrases seemed unequal to the elevation of Church music, but these, compared with the work in its entirety, are as the details of a broadly conceived picture. The enthusiasm of my English friends also fired my zeal to give an interpretation worthy of the great work. Miss Novello and Miss H. Cawse did their best. The "Benedictus" with the heavenly violin solo (Mori), enchanted us all.' A later manuscript copy of the programme of this occasion is preserved with a most interesting collection of programmes and papers relating to Alsager's concerts, in Add. MS. 52347, part of a collection of papers relating to William Ayrton, the founder of *The Harmonicon*, presented to the Museum in 1964 by his descendant, Miss Phyllis Ayrton. This was the only performance of the Missa Solemnis in England before 1846, when the Philharmonic Society gave it on 4 May. It was also performed at the Birmingham Festival the same year, on 28 August, but 'wretchedly mutilated' according to *The Musical Times*.

The Mass had been performed in Alsager's series of concerts for the Queen Square Select Society, which produced a number of surprisingly early performances of difficult works by Beethoven. The concerts were divided into two classes, for the piano and violin. Moscheles was called on again in 1833 to play the two late piano sonatas, opp. 109 and 111. He noted: 'I found some of my hearers listening with deep devotion, whilst at my own house artists seem comparatively indifferent; some certainly are moved, while others are scared by the extravagancies of the master, and do not recover their equanimity until I favour them with the more intelligible D minor Sonata' (op. 31, no. 2).

On 9 March 1845, Moscheles was invited to play an arduous programme of Beethoven sonatas for an occasion entitled 'Offering to Beethoven. High-Priest—M. Moscheles', of which the programme (Plate XV) is preserved in Add. MS. 52347. He played op. 29 (i.e. the D minor sonata, op. 31, no. 2, in the accepted numbering), op. 90, and none other than the Hammerklavier sonata, op. 106. Apparently he was asked for encores as well, for Moscheles's recollection of the recital in his diary reads: 'They made me play four of Beethoven's Sonatas and an Improvisation, and I was glad that my powers did not fail in the B [flat] major sonata. In the Adagio in F sharp minor my feelings were most powerfully moved, but in the fugue it pained me to find so many extravagances. It contains more discords than concords, and Beethoven seems to me all the while to be saying, "I intend working up a subject in a learned manner, it may sound well or not".' It is interesting that the programme of this meeting refers to the Hammerklavier as dedicated to the Archduke Rudolph; this dedication was dropped, for some unexplained reason, from the first English editions of op. 106. At a 'Second Offering to Beethoven' on 6 April 1845, Moscheles played op. 14, nos. 1 and 2, op. 81a, and op. 111.

On both 16 and 30 March 1845, a 'Beethoven Illustrative Party' was given for the Queen Square Select Society (of which the programmes are also in Add. MS. 52347). At each, instead of piano music, there was presented an evening of string quartets at which Beethoven's op. 18, no. 4, op. 74 and op. 132, and, secondly, op. 18, no. 6, op. 95 and op. 135 were played by Sainton, Goffrie, Hill and Rousselot. These were the prelude to another bold experiment by Alsager, the foundation of the Beethoven Quartet Society in 1845, with the object 'of giving the most perfect performance possible of those beautiful Compositions'.

Copies of the prospectus and a complete set of programmes of the first season have been preserved in the
Ayrton collection already mentioned. The 'Preliminary
Ideal', dated 6 January 1845, announced five meetings for
the first season at each of which three quartets would be
performed: one from the early op. 18 set, one from the
middle period, opp. 59, 74, 95, and one of the late quartets.
Membership was limited to fifty at a subscription of five
guineas, and the qualifications for membership were: 'not
only a certain rank or station in Society, but a certain
knowledge and estimation of the compositions of Beethoven'.
These requirements seem to have met with some opposition,
as the revised prospectus, dated 6 March 1845, which
appears to have been the one circulated, omits the qualifications and also the explicit stipulation that the performers,
who would be most carefully selected, 'would be required
to undergo the most careful rehearsals'. However, before
the first meeting of the Beethoven Quartet Society the
Council felt obliged to issue a further Address on 12 April,
defining their aims in detail:

I.   That the composition should be of a highly refined and
intellectual character;

II.   That it should be played by the best artists, prepared by
long practice and careful study of the author's design;

III.   That the performance should be in the presence of an
audience able to appreciate both the composition and its
execution.

The study of the scores of the quartets was earnestly
recommended to both performers and audience, while the
organisers declared themselves satisfied from the applications
they had received of the standing of the audience, 'all will
listen with profound attention'.

After these imposing preliminaries, the first meeting was
held at 8 o'clock on 21 April 1845, at 76 Harley Street,
when quartets op. 18, no. 1, op. 59, no. 3, and op. 127 were
performed. The subsequent meetings of the first season

consisted of: op. 18, no. 3, op. 59, no. 1 and op. 131 (5 May); op. 18, no. 4, op. 74 and op. 132 (19 May); op. 18, nos. 2 and 6, op. 95 and op. 135 (2 June); op. 18, no. 5, op. 59, no. 2 and op. 130 (16 June). Thus all Beethoven's quartets, with the exception of the separate Grosse Fuge, were to be heard in London in 1845. The programmes of the meetings are unusual productions (Plate XVI) with musical incipits, comments on the history of the works, the first performers, and the price Beethoven was paid for them, together with extracts from contemporary critics, and Beethoven's biographers. Quotations from Milton and Shakespeare adorn the programmes, the collected edition of which (published by R. Cocks & Co. in 1846) states that they were selected by the quartet's viola-player, Henry Hill, 'who has shown a rare felicity in establishing the mysterious relation between poetry, or eloquent thoughts in prose (which *are* poetry), and music'. Other performers in the 1845 season were Sainton, Sivori and Vieuxtemps (violins), and Rousselot on the 'cello, who also superintended the rehearsals. Special tribute is given to Rousselot in his role of providing correct texts for the performers: 'Great obstacles were to be overcome in the first instance, in the rescue of Beethoven's Quartetts from obscurity, in consequence of the numerous errors with which all the editions of them abounded'. Rousselot 'succeeded with infinite labour in such a correction, first of the scores and then of the separate parts, that probably not a single fault remained when these copies were employed for the performances of the Beethoven Quartett Society'. Rousselot's parts formed the basis of the edition of the quartets also published by Cocks in 1846. The preface to the collected edition of programmes also contained the enlightened statement that the promoters of the Society 'hoped also to assist in removing some unhappy prejudices, which had spread but too widely, relative to the later works of Beethoven, which were pronounced crude, and wild, and discordant; as indications, in fact, that, with the loss of the faculty of hearing, the monarch of modern musicians had lost the power of producing just harmonies, and works at once truly great and original'. Eight meetings of the Beethoven Quartet Society were apparently held in 1846, although unfortunately the separate series of programmes in the Ayrton collection is not complete. The Beethoven quartets were all repeated and works by Haydn and Mozart were added: 'the subscribers will probably be surprised to find how much additional grandeur and dignity may be imparted to these comparatively simple works, by the style in which they will be performed by the chosen artists of this Society'. At the end of the 1846 season, the promoters, announcing the success of their venture, concluded that it was now time that the management passed to professional musicians and that Rousselot would undertake this.

SELECT BIBLIOGRAPHY

Emily Anderson, *The Letters of Beethoven*, 3 vols., London, 1961.

G. von Breuning, *Aus dem Schwarzspanierhaus*, Vienna, 1874.

A. Carse, 'The Choral Symphony in London', *Music and Letters*, January 1951, pp. 47-58.

H. B. and C. L. E. Cox, *Leaves from the Journals of Sir George Smart*, London, 1907.

O. E. Deutsch, 'Der Liederdichter Reissig', *Neues Beethoven-Jahrbuch*, vi, 1935, pp. 59-65.

M. B. Foster, *History of the Philharmonic Society of London: 1813-1912*, London, 1912.

T. Frimmel, *Beethoven-Handbuch*, 2 vols., Leipzig, 1926.

J. C. Hadden, *George Thomson . . . his Life & Correspondence*, London, 1898.

W. Hess, *Verzeichnis der nicht in der Gesamtausgabe veröffentlichten Werke Ludwig van Beethovens*, Wiesbaden, 1957.

P. Hirsch and C. B. Oldman, 'Contemporary English Editions of Beethoven', *The Music Review*, February 1953, pp. 1-35.

C. Hopkinson and C. B. Oldman, *Thomson's Collections of National Song, with special reference to the contributions of Haydn and Beethoven*, Edinburgh, 1940.

E. Hüffer, *Anton Felix Schindler*, Münster, 1909.

J. Kerman, 'Beethoven Sketchbooks in the British Museum', *Proceedings of The Royal Musical Association*, 93, 1966-67, pp. 77-96.
Ludwig van Beethoven. Autograph Miscellany from circa 1786-1799. British Museum Additional Manuscript 29801, ff. 39-162 (the 'Kafka Sketchbook'), 2 vols. (facsimile and transcription), 1970.

G. Kinsky, *Das Werk Beethovens: thematisch-bibliographisches Verzeichnis . . .*, completed and edited by H. Halm, Munich, 1955.

J. Mewburn Levien, *Beethoven and the Royal Philharmonic Society*, London, 1927.

D. W. MacArdle, 'Beethoven and George Thomson', *Music and Letters*, January 1956, pp. 27-49.

New Beethoven Letters, translated and annotated by D. W. MacArdle and Ludwig Misch, Norman, 1957.

I. Moscheles, *The Life of Beethoven*, 2 vols., London, 1841. (A free translation of A. Schindler, *Biographie*, Münster, 1840, with supplementary material.)

Life of Moscheles with selections from his Diaries and Correspondence by his Wife, translated by A. D. Coleridge, London, 1873.

R. Northcott, *Beethoven's 'Fidelio' in London*, London, 1918.

G. Nottebohm, *Beethoveniana*, Leipzig and Winterthur, 1872.

Zweite Beethoveniana, Leipzig, 1887.

C. B. Oldman, 'Beethoven's Variations on National Themes: their composition and first publication', *The Music Review*, February 1951, pp. 45-51.

B. Schofield, 'Letter of Anton Schindler', *The British Museum Quarterly*, xxi, 2, 1957, pp. 30-1.

J. S. Shedlock, 'Beethoven's Sketch Books', *The Musical Times*, xxxiii, 1892, pp. 331, 394, 461, 523, 589, 649, 717; xxxiv, 1893, pp. 14, 530; xxxv, 1894, pp. 13, 449, 596.

N. Temperley, 'Tempo and Repeats in the Early Nineteenth Century', *Music and Letters*, October 1966, pp. 323-36.

A. W. Thayer, *Chronologisches Verzeichniss der Werke Ludwig van Beethoven's*, Berlin, 1865.

Life of Beethoven, revised and edited by Elliot Forbes, 2 vols., Princeton, 1964.

A. Tyson, 'The Text of Beethoven's op. 61', *Music and Letters*, April 1962, pp. 104-14.

'The Hammerklavier Sonata and its English editions', *The Musical Times*, April 1962, pp. 235-7.

The Authentic English Editions of Beethoven, London, 1963.

'Moscheles and his "Complete Edition" of Beethoven', *The Music Review*, May 1964, pp. 136-41.

'The Textual Problems of Beethoven's Violin Concerto', *The Musical Quarterly*, October 1967, pp. 482-502.

Beethoven. Violin Concerto, Op. 61. A revised edition of the Eulenburg Pocket Score, with introduction, 1968.

'Conversations with Beethoven', *The Musical Times*, January 1970, pp. 25-8.

M. Unger, 'Zu Beethovens Briefwechsel mit B. Schotts Söhnen in Mainz', *Neues Beethoven-Jahrbuch*, iii, 1927, pp. 51-61.

F. Wegeler and F. Ries, *Biographische Notizen über Ludwig van Beethoven*, Coblenz, 1838.

Dagmar Weise, *Beethoven. Ein Skizzenbuch zur Pastoralsymphonie op. 68 und zu den Trios op. 70, 1 und 2*, Beethoven House, Bonn, 1961. Transcription of British Museum Add. MS. 31766, with introduction and notes.

APPENDIX I

MUSIC MANUSCRIPTS
OF BEETHOVEN
IN THE BRITISH MUSEUM

AUTOGRAPH MANUSCRIPTS

Add. MS. 29801
Two groups of sketches, bound together:
ff. 2-37 Sketches for *The Ruins of Athens*, op. 113, and *King Stephen*, op. 117; 1811.
ff. 39-162 Miscellaneous sketches; *c.* 1786-99. (See Bibliography under Kerman.)
Purchased from Johann Nepomuk Kafka, 1875.

Add. MS. 29997
Miscellaneous sketches; 1799-1826.
Purchased from Johann Nepomuk Kafka, 1876.

Add. MS. 47852, f. 2
Two staves only from the top of a page of sketches. The verso may relate to the finale of the string quartet, op. 59, no. 1; 1806?
Bequeathed by Edward Harry William Meyerstein, 1952.

Add. MS. 31766
Sketchbook for the Pastoral symphony, op. 68, and the piano trios, op. 70, nos. 1 and 2; 1808. (See Bibliography under Weise.)
Purchased from Julian Marshall, 1880-81.

Add. MS. 14396, f. 30
Sketches for the first and second movements of the Hammerklavier sonata, op. 106; 1818.
Presented by Vincent Novello, 1843.

Egerton MS. 2795
Pocket sketchbook mainly for the string quartet in B flat, op. 130;
1825.
Purchased through Leo Liepmannssohn at a Berlin sale, 1895.

Add. MS. 38070, ff. 51-2
Sketch for the andante of the string quartet in C sharp minor,
op. 131; 1826.
*Presented by Mrs. Clara Morten in accordance with the wishes of her late
husband, Alfred Morten, 1910.*

Add. MS. 37767
Sonata for violin and piano in G, op. 30, no. 3; 1802.
Bequeathed by Miss Harriet Chichele Plowden, 1907.

Add. MS. 29803, ff. 1-2b
Cadenza for the rondo of Mozart's piano concerto in D minor
(K.466), WoO 58b; 1802-5 or 1808-9.
Purchased from Johann Nepomuk Kafka, 1875.

Add. MS. 47852
ff. 5-11   'Lied aus der Ferne', WoO 137; 1809.
ff. 13-14b   'Der Liebende', WoO 139; 1809.
Bequeathed by Edward Harry William Meyerstein, 1952.

Egerton MS. 2327
Themes for twelve folksong variations for piano and flute, op. 105,
nos. 1, 2, 4-6; op. 107, nos. 1, 2, 4, 5, 8-10, with a few sketches for
the variations; 1818.
Purchased from L. Bihn, 1873.

COPIES WITH AUTOGRAPH ANNOTATIONS

Add. MS. 41631
Drei Sonaten fürs Klavier, WoO 47, the three early piano sonatas
in E flat, F minor and D; 1783. *Printed* copy with a few autograph
annotations.
Presented by Edward Perry Warren, 1928.

Egerton MS. 2727
The Mount of Olives, op. 85; *c.* 1804-11. Full score.
Purchased from Emanuel Nowotny, 1889.

Add. MS. 41630, ff. 1-41
Piano solo part of the Triple Concerto, op. 56; *c.* 1807.
Presented by Edward Perry Warren, 1928.

Add. MS. 47851
Concerto, op. 61, piano and violin versions; 1808. Full score.
Bequeathed by Edward Harry William Meyerstein, 1952.

British Museum Loan 4 (Royal Philharmonic Society)
MS. 518   Overture to *The Ruins of Athens*, op. 113; 1815.
            Full score.
MS. 519   Overture, *Namensfeier*, op. 115; 1815. Full score.
MS. 520   Overture to *King Stephen*, op. 117; 1815. Full
            score.
MS. 521   Overture, *Die Weihe des Hauses*, op. 124; 1822.
            Full score.
MS. 21   Ninth symphony, op. 125; 1824. Full score.

APPENDIX II

LETTERS, DOCUMENTS
AND MISCELLANEA

Add. MSS. 35263-9 *passim*
Correspondence with George Thomson of Edinburgh; 1803-19.
Most of Beethoven's letters are *signed* copies.
Purchased from Mrs Sinclair Thomson, 1899.

Add. MS. 33965
f. 170   Letter to Joseph von Varena of Graz; 8 February
     1812.
f. 172   Letter to Robert Birchall; 28 October 1815.
f. 174   Receipt to Franz Christian Kirchhoffer for £50 for
     the ninth symphony; 27 April 1824. *Signed.*
f. 175   Letter to Baron Ignaz von Gleichenstein; 23 June
     1807.
f. 177   Letter to Karl van Beethoven; 25 August 1825.
f. 178   Letter to Karl Czerny; [1818].
f. 179   Letter to Anton Schindler?; 1823.
*Presented by Andrew George Kurtz, Secretary of the Liverpool Philharmonic
Society, 1891.*

Add. MS. 29804
f. 10   Letter to Baron Ignaz von Gleichenstein; summer
     1808.
f. 13   Letter to Dr Dorner; February 1809.
Purchased from Johann Nepomuk Kafka, 1875.

Add. MS. 41628
f. 28   Letter to Georg Friedrich Treitschke; summer 1814.

ff. 30-5b   Three letters to Adolf Martin Schlesinger; 13, 14
November 1821, 9 April 1822.

Presented by Edward Perry Warren, 1928.

Add. MS. 52337B
Letter to Baron Johann Pasqualati; [*c.* 1816?]. This brief note was
acquired after the publication of Emily Anderson's edition and the
text is accordingly given here. Baron Pasqualati assisted Beethoven
on business matters and allowed him to live in rooms in his own
house on the Mölkerbastei. Beethoven lived there on and off from
1804 to 1815. The note was written after Beethoven had moved
out but was still in touch with Baron Pasqualati. Other similar
notes have been preserved from 1816.

Theuerster Freund!
Ich bitte Sie mir zu wissen zu machen, wann ich morgen
Vor oder Nachmittag Sie [*sic*] einige Augenblicke sprechen
kann, ich werde Ihnen so wenig als möglich Zeit rauben,
einmal besuchte ich Sie schon. Sie waren aber nicht zu Hause.
Wie immer
Ihr Freund
L. v. Beethoven.
(Dearest Friend,
I beg you to let me know when I can speak to you for a
few moments tomorrow morning or afternoon. I will take
up as little of your time as possible. I called once already but
you were not at home.
As ever,
Your Friend
L. v. Beethoven.)

Presented by Miss Phyllis Ayrton, 1964.

Add. MS. 41295, f. 131
Letter to the family of Cajetan Giannatasio Del Rio; 1817.

Presented by Mrs Florence Julia Street, 1925.

Egerton MS. 3097B, f. 2
Fragment of a letter to Nanette Streicher; [January 1818]. The
remainder of the letter is in the Beethoven House, Bonn.

Purchased from Mrs L. J. Edwards, 1933.

Add. MS. 38071, f. 29
Receipt for his half year's pension of 600 gulden from the Kinsky
treasury in Prague; 25 September 1825. *Signed.*

*Presented by Mrs. Clara Morten in accordance with the wishes of her late
husband, Alfred Morten, 1910.*

Loan 48. 13/3
f. 27   Letter to Karl Holz; summer 1826.
f. 28   Tracing(?) of Beethoven's letter to Ferdinand Wolanek;
               1825. The original is in the Beethoven House, Bonn.
f. 29   Tracing(?) of a letter of Wolanek to Beethoven, with
               an autograph scrawl by Beethoven; 1825. The orig-
               inal is in the Beethoven House, Bonn.

Add. MS. 29260, f. 1
Letter to William Ehlers; 1 August 1826. *Copy.*

In a manuscript purchased at Sotheby's, 12 July 1872.

MISCELLANEA

Add. MS. 38794, f. 155
Estimate by George Thomson of the cost of publishing three
sonatas with violin accompaniment and three string quintets by
Beethoven; January 1810. A similar undated, but later, estimate
for publishing three quintets is in the Thomson correspondence,
Add. MS. 35263, f. 314.

Purchased from Walter V. Daniell, 1913.

Loan 48
Official papers of the Royal Philharmonic Society. The following
items relate to Beethoven:

Loan 48. 2/1-2, 3/1
Directors' Minute Books, 1816-37, and General Minute Book,
1813-54, contain some references to Beethoven.

Loan 48. 13/10, f. 181
Letter of Domenico Dragonetti to the Philharmonic Society
relating to the ninth symphony; 21 January 1825.

Loan 48. 13/32, ff. 12, 18
Letters of Sir George Smart to the Philharmonic Society relating
to the ninth symphony; 12 March 1825, 22 January 1828.

Loan 48. 14/1
Lock of Beethoven's hair; 1827.

Loan 48. 14/2
Half a laurel leaf from one of the wreaths thrown on Beethoven's grave; 1827. Another leaf is in Egerton MS. 3097B.

Loan 48. 14/3
Miscellaneous papers relating to Beethoven, including copies of letters of Ferdinand Ries to Beethoven on behalf of the Society, 1817, papers relating to the financial assistance given to Beethoven, including autograph letters of Moscheles, 1827, Paul Friedrich Walther's invitation card to Beethoven's funeral, appeals to the Society for support for Beethoven's memorial at Bonn, 1837, etc., with papers relating to Mme Fanny Linzbauer's gift on 17 December 1870, of the bust of Beethoven by Schaller, 1859-71, etc.

Loan 48. 14/8
Photograph of Beethoven's last letter to Moscheles, in the hand of Schindler but *signed* by Beethoven eight days before his death; 18 March 1827. With a list of metronome markings relating to the ninth symphony.

Add. MSS. 41771-9, 42225, *passim*
Papers of Sir George Smart. References to Beethoven are in Add. MSS. 41771, 41779, papers relating to the Philharmonic Society, 41772, 42225, memoranda books, and 41774, journal of his tour of Germany in 1825.

Presented by Hugh Bertram Cox, C.B., 1929, 1931.

Department of Printed Books, Case 61.h.2. and K.6.d.3
Collection of programmes annotated by Sir George Smart.

Add. MS. 29260
ff. 2, 3   Two draft letters of Johann Andreas Stumpff, instrument-maker of London, to Johann B. Streicher of Vienna, asking for an autograph of Beethoven, and sending a set of Arnold's edition of Handel as a gift for Beethoven; 1822, 1826.

f. 4   Draft letter from Stumpff to Beethoven introducing Sir George Smart and mentioning Stumpff's fruitless efforts to obtain satisfaction from the Royal Household regarding the Battle symphony; 1825.

Purchased at Sotheby's, 12 July 1872.

Add. MS. 52347
Papers and programmes relating to the Beethoven Quartet Society, etc.; 1845, etc.

Presented by Miss Phyllis Ayrton, 1964.

Add. MS. 46839L
Letter of Anton Schindler to Charles Neate relating to the possible acquisition by the British Museum of Schindler's Beethoven collection; 6 August 1845.

Purchased from Heinrich Eisemann, 1948.

INDEX

71

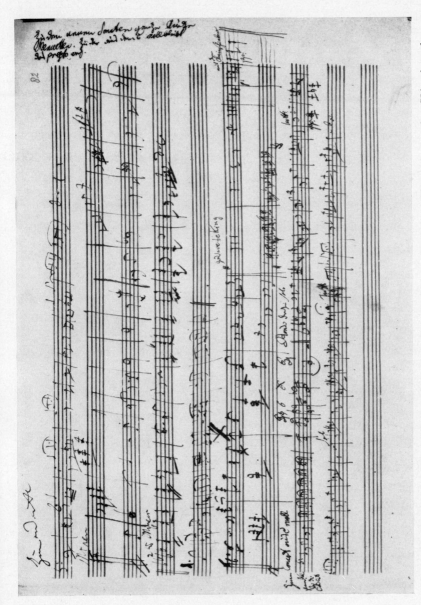

1 Notes relating to the piano sonatas, op. 10, sketches of 'God Save the King' and the piano concerto, op. 37, c.1797

11   Sketches for the Adagio of an unfinished piano concerto, *c.*1790

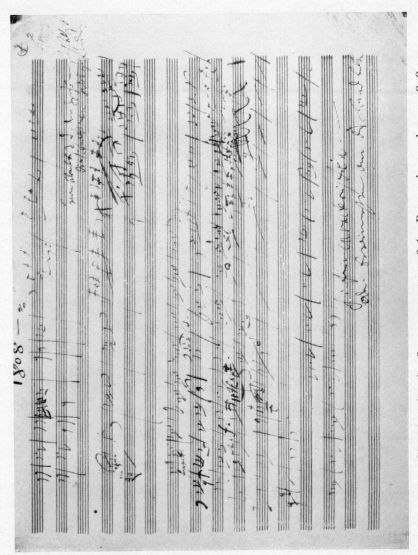

III   Sketches for the first movement of the Pastoral symphony, 1808

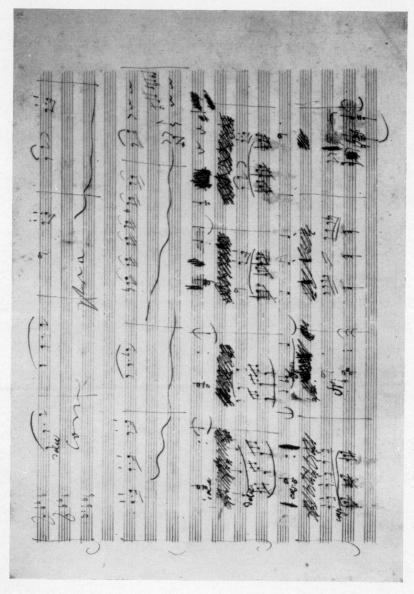

IV Autograph of the violin sonata, op. 30, no. 3, showing corrections to the Tempo di Minuetto, 1802

v Portrait of George Thomson. From the water-colour by William Nicholson in the Scottish National Portrait Gallery

Estimate   Jan.y 1810.—

Suppose I pay to M. B. for three Sonatas w.t a
Violin accomp.t _____ £40. „ „

And for Engraving these _____ 20. „ „
                                                ————————
                                                  £60. „ „

If these are sold at 10/6 — I find the paper
and printing will cost 3 Sh. and M.r Pres-
-ton must have a profit of 4 Sh. which
would leave me 3/6 clear for each copy:
Thus to indemnify myself I must sell
350 copies, which at 3/6 each amounts
to £61. 2. 6. — But the expence of adver-
-tising would require selling 60 copies
more, that is, in all 410 copies.

Suppose I pay to M. B. for three Quintettos, for
Violins &.c _____ £40. „ „

And for engraving these _____ 37. „ „
                                                ————————
                                                  £77. „ „

If these are sold at 15 Sh. — I conceive
the paper and printing will cost 5/6,
and that M.r Preston will demand
5/6, which would leave me 4 Sh.—
clear for each copy: And thus to
indemnify myself I must sell 390
copies, which at 4/6 each amounts
to £78. „ „ — And for advertising
I w.d need to sell 50 copies more, that
is, in all 440 copies.

VI   George Thomson's estimate of the cost of publishing violin
sonatas and string quintets by Beethoven, 1810

Monsieur!

On m'assurent que vous ne me refuserez pas, de me faire payer, chez Messieurs Fries & Comp, au lieu de 3 # en or, 4 # en or pour chaque chanson, j'ai rendu les 9 Chansons, a Susdites Messieurs, j'aurois ainsi encore 9 # en or a recevoir.

Haydn même m'assuré, qu'il a aussi reçu pour chaque chanson 4# en or, et pourtant il n'écrivit que pour le Clavecin et un Violon toute seule sans Ritornel & Violoncelle &c. Quant a Monsieur Kozeluch, que vous livre chaque chanson avec accompagnement pour &c je vous félicite beaucoup et aussi aux auditeurs angloises & écossais &c quand ils en goutent. Moi je m'estime encore une fois plus supérieur en ce Genre que Monsieur Kozeluch j Miserabilis j et j'espere croyant, que vous possedes quelque distinction, laquelle vous mette en état, de me rendre justice.

Je n'ai pas encore reçu la reponse a ma lettre dernière, et je souhaite de savoir a quoi que je suis avec vous. Vous auriez déjà longtems les 3 Sonates pour 100 # en or et les 3 Quintettes pour la même somme, mais je ne peux rien risquer en cette affaire, et il faut que je reçoive les sommes fixées des Messieurs Fries, en presentent les Exemplaires.

A ce qui regard les 12 Chansons, avec le texte angloise le honoraire est 70 # en or. Pour la Cantate, contenant la Bataille dans le mer baltique 60 # en or, pour l'oratoire je demande 600 # en or, mais il est nécessaire, que le texte doit singulierement bien fait, je vous prie instantement d'aejoindre toujours le texte aux chansons écossais. je ne comprends pas comme vous, qui vous êtes Connoisseur, ne pouviez comprendre, que je procurois des Compositions, tout a fait autres, si j'aurai le texte a la main, et les chansons ne peuvent jamais obtenir des produits parfaits, si vous ne m'envoyés pas le texte, et vous m'obligeré's a la fin de refuser vos ordres ulterieurs.

VII   Letter of Beethoven to George Thomson, 29 February 1812.
Signed copy

VIII   Title-page of Thomson's *Twelve National Airs*, London, 1819

IX   Portrait of Muzio Clementi, from his *Gradus ad Parnassum*,
London, *c*.1830

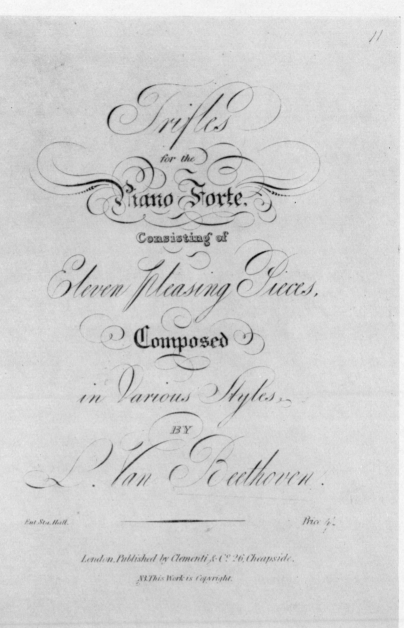

x Title-page of Clementi's edition of Beethoven's *Bagatelles*, op. 119, London, 1823

XI Title-page of *Drei Sonaten fürs Klavier*, [1783], with an auto-graph note by Beethoven

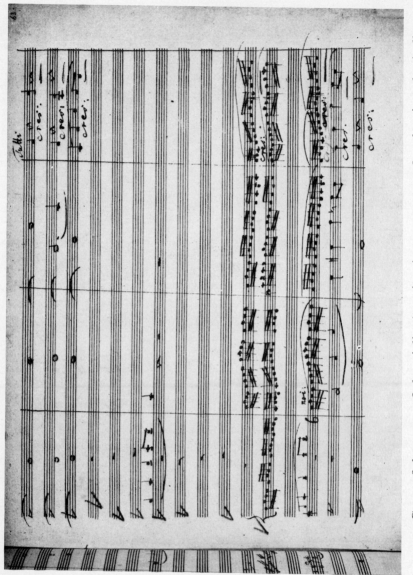

XII   Copy of the score of the violin (or piano) concerto, op. 61, showing the 'cello passage omitted from the first edition, 1808

XIII   Portrait of Sir George Smart. From the oil painting by
William Bradley in the National Portrait Gallery

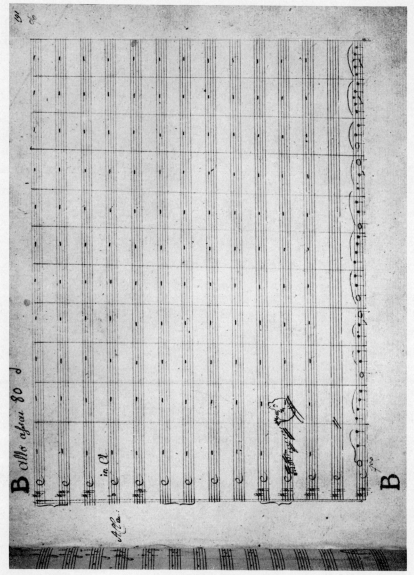

xiv Copy of the score of the ninth symphony sent to the Philharmonic Society, with a conductor's memorandum, 1824

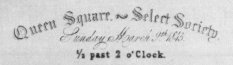

xv   Programme of the Queen Square Select Society's
      'Offering to Beethoven,' 9 March 1845

xvi Programme of the Beethoven Quartet Society, 16 June 1845. Two states: (*a*) the original litho-graphic publication of 1845; (*b*) the reprint, from engraved plates, of 1846

(*a*)

(*b*)